EMPOWERING CHILDREN

EMPOWERING CHILDREN

Jon Merritt

Author of
A Parent's Primer

Parenting
Resources
PUBLICATIONS

Merritt, Jon
    Empowering Children: A Parent's Guide to Building-In
    Success and Self-esteem

    1. Parenting Skills. 2. Child Psychology.
    3. Child Development. 4. Counseling Methods.

ISBN: 1-880360-01-2 (paper)

Design, layout and typesetting
by Paul John Pastor

TABLE OF CONTENTS

To Cathy, my wife and best friend.

Acknowledgements

Thanks to the parents and students of Alameda Elementary School in Portland, Oregon, whose hard work, love and dedication to each other has taught me so much; to my children Karin, 21, Justin, 20, and Shannon, 14, for their love, support and wonderful spirits; to my buddy Russ Zachmeyer for his good advice and affection; and to friends and colleagues Susan Isaacs, Rosy Taylor and Carolyn Sheldon for their encouragement and mentoring over the years.

Introduction

ABOUT THIS BOOK

You have probably noticed the many books and articles written in the past ten years or more on the subjects of child-raising, discipline, and communication. I've read many of them and have recommended some of the better ones to parents of the children I work with. However, I saw very little evidence that the ideas and suggestions in those books were translated into action by those parents and I wondered why parents read the books and changed their behavior so little. After all, my expectations were fairly limited — I hoped that some of the good ideas might rub off enough to help in even one instance.

I began to find an answer to this question several years ago as I gave the same prescription "try this, try that" approach in the parent classes I taught. I received class evaluations which said almost nothing about the advice and technical aspects of parenting skills but spoke enthusiastically about the change in their underlying attitudes. Here are some comments culled from recent evaluations:

- "I feel more like I'm in charge now and I feel better about myself."

- "I'm not so defensive and ready to jump at the first provocation."

- "Just realizing that I didn't have to control everything

in my family was the best part."

- "Knowing I'm not the only one with the problem was the most useful for me."

- "The fact that I have been able to calm down and thus defuse a tense situation has been wonderful."

- "The perspective I have now has helped me to see the situation in a more adult way and then respond reasonably."

Parents were telling me that the suggestions were working because *their attitude about themselves and their children were changing,* from being worried and guilty and unsure to becoming more optimistic, more objective, and more confident. Those new ways of seeing themselves and their families bred success in the things they were working on and the success bred further confidence.

Two letters I received from parents may illustrate how this change took place:

"Dear Jon,

I really appreciate the help you've given us in dealing with _____'s resistance and back talking. What has helped most, I guess, is my own self-control at the starting point. Just reminding myself to stay calm, stay in the adult and then use the most minimal response (like 'uh, huh' or 'umm' or 'oh?') has worked well because it apparently sends a message to _____ that it's okay, Dad's not upset, he's in control, he can help. Makes me feel good, too!
Also, you validated my own thoughts about firm, consistent limits being the best way to teach responsibility. I felt like I was on the right track after all. Also, your 'shoot for 80 percent of the time' being in

good control has helped me relax and be human, too. *Funny thing, the more relaxed I am, the easier it is to do those things. The last thing I can think of is your insistence on seeing the reason behind the behavior. When I can do that, it always makes me a little less prone to shoot my mouth off and make things worse. I end up feeling better about my own competence as a parent. It sort of builds positive like that, you know?*
Thanks a lot! You also made this process kind of fun, too, like a puzzle to figure out. I'll call if we get stuck.

Sincerely,"

Another letter commented more on the important issue of specific skills learned as well as the parent's underlying self-concept:

"Dear Jon,

You asked me to drop you a note after a month for an update on our progress with the chores hassle. The most valuable things have been the ideas of communication and how to help kids solve their own problems.

We've been really working on responding to the kids in a way that allows them to feel they are being taken seriously and that their feelings are important. It's been quite a change for us - from dictators and resentful little creeps to listeners and more cooperative little humans. Not perfect, of course, but much better. It sure is hard to break that habit! But we're seeing a lot less arguing now around chores, thank heaven. I was about to head for the coast, without them!

The problem-solving ideas have also worked. _____ fought my throwing his own problems back at him for a while. I guess he was too used to me solving them for him but now he's getting the idea that Mom won't budge and he does what he's supposed to (most of the time). Last week he tried to get me hooked into his homework problem. *'I can't do this, I don't have the right books. I can't make these charts...' and on and on. I said, 'Sounds like you've got a problem,' instead of my usual, 'Oh, don't gripe, just sit down and do it' routine for a half hour. He just looked at me and said, 'No kidding' and went into his room and started on it! I could have done a little dance.*

Anyhow, hope this updates you. Thanks."

Feedback such as these letters and similar reports by phone and in person were teaching me which concepts stayed longest and worked best.

Then I began to refocus my discussions with individual parents when consulting with them on school-related or home behavior problems, concentrating heavily on empowering them, giving them perspective, trying to nurture a more forgiving, accepting view of themselves as well as their children. Without changes in these wellsprings of motivation, no amount of prescriptive advice would be of much use. As I became more effective at this sort of encouragement, more parents would tell me that things were changing for the better at home.

No wonder the books alone won't do it. Consider for a moment the array of factors that complicate even a simple interaction within a family system: your own nurturing, or lack of it, as a child; the way your parents communicated, or didn't; your own birth order; the birth order of your children; your spouse's family background; your "born that way" personality; how much money you make, or don't make; your neighborhood; your religion; the fact that it is 1992 and not 1952; what you ate for breakfast; your job; what time it is;... I hope you are beginning to understand why behavior change on your part and your child's part cannot be addressed very adequately on a surface level.

Something else seemed to be getting in the way,

something subtle but powerful that didn't surface until I got to know parents well and they began to trust me. It's what I began to call the "Everybody else seems to have it all together as a family and I don't and I feel rotten" syndrome. It is as if parents believe that "Family Ties" and "The Cosby Show" ("Father Know Best" or "Leave it to Beaver" in my childhood) is how most families are and should be. As much as I like the positive modeling and messages given to us by these T.V. programs, nothing is further from the truth. Here's the truth that parents whom I talk with seem to love to hear: Family life with children is a gritty, messy, contentious and sometimes marvelously satisfying business. <u>Nobody</u> has is "all together" — if they say so they're probably lying and if you think so, you're kidding yourself. It is a constant struggle to give love in a world that doesn't encourage it, to produce justice in a world that refuses to recognize it, to transmit values in a setting that has eroded most values, to nurture sane, reasonable people in a world that often seems rather insane. That everyone is struggling is a dirty, little secret which when exposed, makes us smile! Then we relax and go about the business of raising our children without always looking over our shoulder.

This book came about because of the feedback parents have given me over the years about what works, what doesn't work, and why. Years of being immersed in families — my own and thousands of others — has made me sensitive to the need for us to always be working on the roots of our behavior as well as on the leaves and branches; that is, our underlying attitudes and feelings as well as the specific techniques and skills that we have to be practicing. I have tried to help you do that in this book.

As with any book you would pick up from the self-help section of the bookstore, this one is no cure-all, nor does it address all issues and all ages. It is intended primarily for parents of children ages five through twelve (elementary school) whose development has been basically normal — meaning that they have no seriously debilitating physical, intellectual or emotional problems that get in the way of their day-to-day functioning. Teenagers will respond to most of the communication skills you will learn but discipline with teenagers requires different and somewhat more sophisticated responses than are generally used with preteen children.

Your changing of behavior and attitudes requires some hard work. You may need to read, talk to friends or professionals, reread, set up plans, get discouraged and give up and then try again. But I think this book will get you started because it addresses some of the most basic issues: surviving daily life with children, teaching respect, fostering self-esteem, learning to value others, sharing power and what it means to love a child. You can teach your children to be responsible, humane adults and enjoy them while you're doing it.

EMPOWERING CHILDREN

CHAPTER 1: POWER

For the past twenty-five years I have been working with children and their parents, helping them to negotiate an increasingly complex maze of everyday life. It is a difficult task to raise a responsible, capable child and retain your own self-esteem and perspective as a parent. What has impressed me most through all of this is the desire of parents, regardless of their external circumstances, to do a good job of raising their children. I've been equally impressed with the children's desire to grow up to be healthy and independent. Those desires on the parts of everyone in a family have a profound effect on how the game of growing up is played out. I believe that these needs to "do it right" create the dynamic force behind both the successful and positive things and the misguided, potentially destructive things that happen along the way.

A fact you may have to accept on faith right now is that *your child is doing the best she knows how* with the tools she has. Beneath even the most difficult, resistive behavior, there is a strong desire to be independent, successful and respected. What appears to be bothersome, pointless behavior is nearly always a striving to be good. As you become better at analyzing behavior and responding effectively to it, you will begin to see the truth in this contention.

And as you begin to act on this belief, with the trust that it implies in children's capabilities, you will see your faith turned into positive change. It's a marvelous process to observe!

THE PAYOFFS OF EMPOWERMENT

A first grade child I have recently been seeing in a group is a good example of what is being described here. Megan (not her real name) came to school from a home severely disrupted by a divorce and constant drug use, which got so destructive that she was removed by the state and placed in her grandparents' home. Megan would not smile, refused offers to play with other children, would not try to do her work and, in fact, showed almost no facial reaction to anything, good or bad. She occasionally would disappear from the playground and turn up later at her grandparents' house. The grandmother, teacher and I soon met to plan how to begin the task of teaching Megan that she had the intelligence and ability to interact with others and succeed in school and to lay the groundwork for the trust in herself and others that would allow her to show her feelings again.

Acting on our belief that underneath the fear and resistance lay a strong desire to be happy and feel competent, here is what we did that seems to have worked successfully:

1. We introduced her to a group of three other girls of the same age whom I was seeing each week during Friday reading period and told her she was welcome to join us. She was terribly shy about that and said no at first but we told her she could come once and see if she liked it enough to come back. It was okay if she did and okay if she did not. She came to the first session and decided she wanted to continue. I focused the group gently on awareness of their own strengths and taught basic social and interaction skills. There was also time for play with

clay and other art media and for free play with dolls and other toys. After a month, I saw the first full smile from Megan and I was elated. I felt that we were now on our way!

2. We developed a plan for home which included the kinds of direct, humane methods of communication and discipline that you will learn in this book. Megan received straight, honest messages instead of the harsh, demeaning and obviously frightful ones she had received in her parents' home. She learned to take responsibility for her chores and her behavior and although she resisted strongly at first (she felt incapable of it), she gradually learned that she could do chores, be on time and respond less catastrophically to frustration. Megan's grandparents should have a medal of honor for their persistence and compassion, especially since these ways of talking, listening and rule-enforcing were not at all familiar to them.

3. The classroom plan was managed by a skilled and understanding teacher who allowed Megan at first to look and listen and participate only as she wanted to. Gradually, Megan's teacher (after being sure there was some trust between the two) put appropriate demands on her to perform and behave properly. We felt that success in class was crucial and it turned out that we were correct.

After working with Megan for about four months, I arrived at her classroom door to pick her up for group and she met me with tears and a long face.
"Hi, Megan," I said, "You're pretty sad today."
Nods her head.
"What's going on?" I asked.
"I don't want to go," she said, head down and still in

tears.

"That's okay. You don't have to if you don't want to. Any special reason?"

"I want to stay here. I'm reading."

I said, "Well I think that's a great idea. I don't want you to miss that either. And, you can change your mind, too. If you decide you want to keep coming, let me know, okay?"

I gave her a hug and she went back into her classroom. When her teacher and I met later that day, she asked about Megan's refusal to go; was it all right for her to "drop" the group? As we talked, I realized what had been happening and it was exciting: Megan felt strong and she wanted simply to do what kids are supposed to do in first grade — learn to read. Her process of change from afraid and unresponsive to more confident and open had been steady and unspectacular. But all of a sudden (it seemed) we saw a child confident and self-aware enough to say by her action, "I'm ready to get on with the real business of being seven. I want to be like everybody else and read and play and talk to my friends." She told us that our work was over for now.

In our follow-up meeting, Megan's grandparents, her teachers and I agreed that her work was done and she was feeling much better about herself. What had happened in the four months? Plenty. Here is the list we made:

• She received strong, positive messages, from a respected, neutral adult (me) and from her friends in the group, that she was worthy of being included, of being a friend, of being listened to, of making her own decisions.

• She received those same good messages from her teacher by her teacher's respecting her need to just watch at first and then by gradually demanding more from

Megan. I thought the most important step was when she realized she could read like everybody else. It's difficult or impossible for adults to imagine the impact of that on her self-esteem but I would bet it's profound. The teacher is one who also uses positive communication and discipline skills. She brought Megan gradually to the realization of her own power to learn.

• Part way through our work with Megan, her mother finally disappeared from her life; the effect of that was actually positive because of the mother's continuing addiction and unreliability. The grandparents had a chance to calm the level of fear and disruption that Megan had found overwhelming and to replace it with stability and hope.

In short, Megan was *empowered*: the important adults in her world structured her life and communicated with her in ways that made her feel important and capable, by making sure that she experienced success in her personal, social, and educational settings. That happens only if we accept a child's need to be powerful and give the kinds of firm, loving messages that allow them to feel it.

The strength of the need to be autonomous — that is, exercising control over the aspects of your life you need to control — is amazing. Last summer I spent a day in the educational section of a nonprofit organization that trains and educates developmentally disabled children and adults, some of whom are quite severely handicapped, physically and mentally. I visited all the classes and watched the gym teacher as she taught the various age groups, watched people learning to walk or reason or crawl or respond. Soon it occurred to me that I was hearing the same thing from several teachers about "can't" and "won't."

Given the state of some of the children's profound retardation, it appeared to me to be all "can't." I was wrong.

As I sat watching a boy, whom I will call Jack, try to put cupcake holders into the cupcake pan, his teacher looked at me and said, "He can do it but he just doesn't want to." This boy couldn't even talk, he will never live independently, and yet, as typical as any seventh grader, he was resisting what his teacher wanted him to do. I asked my friend Jim, who runs the organization, if that resistive behavior was unusual in these clients. He said, no, that it was the norm there and a fact that few "outsiders" ever consider as a problem when working with those as disabled as the children in his school.

Later I asked Jack's teacher if I could try something and she agreed. "Jack," I said, "I saw you on a video tape last night at Jim's house. I was impressed with how well you did in stopping and starting the train. You're a pretty capable guy," all this with my hand on his shoulder.

Jack looked at me, his mouth slightly open and his eyes more knowing than I would ever have suspected. He turned back to his table and after a bit of fooling around, put the paper cups into the the tray in short order.

His teacher checked her stopwatch and recorded the time with a knowing smile.

Obviously this all made me think about children whose I.Q.'s are twice that of Jack's. Such children are sometimes cornered into acting as if they are incapable. If the need to be personally powerful and capable is so strong in even the most disabled of us, then it seems to me that we must always take it into account and find many ways to transfer power and responsibilities to children as soon as they can handle it.

A person's healthy need for control will often

masquerade as stubborn resistance and/or feigned incompetence if it is not allowed by the important people in that person's life. What causes a parent to thwart that need? It is usually: 1) underestimation of the child's true ability, 2) the honest bid for personal power is threatening, or 3) the parent is emotionally unable to accept and nurture the need. My eight year old friend Kurt is a good example. Kurt's older brother and father made it nearly impossible for Kurt to take part in either play, talking or arguing in any healthy way. They bulldozed Kurt into acquiescing to what they wanted or bullied him into silence when he raised his voice in protest. Kurt's response was to "go underground" — he became resistive and sneaky. His large reserve of unexpressed anger affected his school behavior. His ability to laugh and smile went away along with any outward displays of anger, but the surreptitious kicking and hitting and refusal to obey the teacher increased. When I got involved with Kurt, it was difficult to get any reaction out of him beyond the nod of his head and a few words. Since Kurt's father was emotionally unavailable at that time as a helper, his mother, teacher and I made a plan for Kurt last year that has continued until the present, helping Kurt to express his feelings and take control over decisions at school and home that will bring his legitimate bids for power back to the "surface." Right now he spends part of each group session with me drawing, painting, playing and making clay objects with one theme: his own (the object he makes or draws) omnipotence and destructive power. His play objects strangle, stab, blow-up, "nuke", shoot, bite hit, kick, and burn-up all rivals, even benign ones. He is the King of Exterminators.

Recently his mother and I talked about Kurt's progress. I described how much happier and responsive he was in school this year and told her about the persisting, violent fantasies in his play. She felt that it was time for the next step, that of involving his father in helping Kurt give up his obsession with power. She asked me to explain to his father what she finally came to realize — people with either too much power (spoiled, over-protected children) or too little power (children with autocratic parents) become obsessed with power. Since Kurt's father has been in therapy for some months we feel very hopeful that Kurt's normal desire to have a say in his life will be acknowledged and nurtured by such an important person.

LEARNING HOW TO EMPOWER CHILDREN

Imagine your child's energy, intelligence and will to be independent as a deep, fast-flowing river, a current hard to stop or tame.

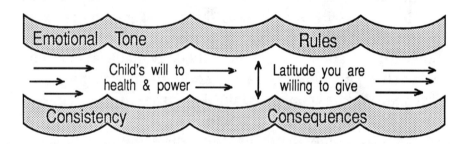

You could stop the river by building a dam. (Some parents try!) A lake would back up behind it and you no longer would have a vital and creative flow of water. You simply can't do that to a child's energy and positive thrust of will — you would end up with either a passive and resentful lake behind the dam or such a strong backlog of resistance that it would burst the dam and flow destructively on its own, unchecked course. I doubt that any healthy parent would care to live with either sort of child.

What you can and must do is accept the fact that the "water" will flow, that it should be strong and deep, but that it must be properly channeled and protected by strong dikes. You determine the width between the dikes (how much latitude in behavior the child is to have) and the thickness of the dikes (the *rules* and the *consistency* with which you enforce the *consequences* and the *emotional tone* surrounding the entire interaction.)

As you learn to set reasonable rules, enforce them without becoming vindictive and shrill, talk and listen to your children in a way that conveys respect, and allow them to experience real-world consequences of their actions, you will notice that their ability to perform will grow and their good feelings about themselves (their self-esteem) will multiply. Empowerment = high self-esteem and it is automatic. All the aspects of a child's life — home, school, peers, social groups — have an effect on self-esteem but yours is greatest. You will affect it by how you talk to, listen to and guide your child, mostly in small, everyday ways. These skills are fairly easy to learn. Over the next few weeks as you read this book and practice new behavior, your attitude towards yourself, your children and misbehavior will change. The way you talk and act toward your children in difficult situations will change. You will find yourself becoming more in control and less emotional when handling day-to-day child raising issues. Once that happens, you won't want to go back to doing it the old way!

BLINDED (OR AT LEAST MYOPIC) BY LOVE

I once knew a boy named Billy, a bright, pleasant first grader who had his own resentful but persistent slave.

Every morning his slave would wake him up, pull the covers off, and drag him to a sitting position. If Billy didn't particularly feel like it, he wouldn't get his school clothes on and the slave would come back (more resentful this time), pull Billy's pajamas off, and put his clothes on him. The slave even carried Billy downstairs to breakfast a few times! Billy had it pretty good for a while until the slave got fed up and learned that he really didn't have to do all those things that a six-year-old is capable of doing.

As you may have guessed, Billy's slave was his Dad. When he came to talk to me he wasn't angry — just very puzzled as to why his son seemed so slow and uncooperative at home and in school. He cares a lot about this otherwise delightful child, but over the years since his birth, Dad and Mom lost sight of the fact that there were many things Billy could do all by himself, without reminders, arguments, slow-down strikes and tears. I asked Billy's parents to think of each daily "episode" in their child's life — the morning routine, homework, chores, bedtime routine — as having a point value, all of them adding up to 100 points. They assigned 50 points to morning routine and divided the rest among the other issues. So, it was a big issue, primarily because it had become a major source of frustration for the parents and a source of tension in the family.

Then I asked them to divide the 50 points of "morning routine" among the various family members according to the effort and emotional energy they expended on this issue. After a long and thoughtful mulling over, Dad gave himself 40 points and Billy 10. Mom had 0 because she was always getting baby sister ready. I asked, "How many points should you and Billy have over this issue?"

Dad said, "Well, I suppose it should be reversed. He's the one who needs to do all those things. I only need to be around to help."

A perceptive Dad when he took the time to consider it. He even gave himself 50 points on the days he provided transportation downstairs!

I asked, "What makes you think this problem of Billy's will ever be solved if you insist on taking 40 or 50 points every day?

He answered, "It won't be."

There are two reasons why Dad is right. I know very few children or adults who wouldn't gladly give up a tedious, repetitive or unpleasant task to someone else if that person insisted every day upon taking it. Would you let me pay you income tax for you? May I clean your garage every month? And I'd bet you would be increasingly willing to let me do these tasks for you if I gave you subtle messages every day that you weren't capable of doing them. You'd also resent me after a while. This creates the second reason why the problem won't be solved — after months or years of living with the implicit message that they are not capable of handling the problem, children will become exactly what we tell them they are.

In the case of the 50-point morning routine, your involvement as a parent should be worth about 5 or 10 points because you can legitimately remind or you can help if asked, and you also need to get somewhere or do something on time. But that is all — the rest is the child's business; the power is his or hers to use to accomplish the task.

We forget that our children are very powerful. A recent incident from my own life illustrates this.

My daughter, Karin, is a strong, intelligent child and is little trouble and much joy. Why, then, would I do such a silly thing as I did last month? She wandered into the living room with a messy-looking bowl of yogurt. I said irritably, "Karin, what are you doing? You know that stuff..." Her look stopped me in mid-sentence. I realized that this was not that little girl with the delightful, fiesty way of trashing a house she once had. But the time...! I thought, such a short time ago that I held her in one hand. That moment is clearer to me than many which happened yesterday.

I apologized to her. I said, "Karin, I'm sorry. Parents have a way of forgetting the passage of time when their kids are concerned. I won't do that again."

We love and we care, so much so that sometimes we don't see that which is happening before our eyes. Our children grow intelligent and more capable, they become wise and more independent and they know it. When we fail to pay our respects to that growing competence and judgment at every phase and stage, we send them a message they must resist, since they are healthy and know they are loved. They act it out. They tell us by their behavior: foot dragging, refusal to do certain things, "forgetting," arguing endlessly about trivia. The point is, for them, to try to get that power back from you little by little, and they do it in the best way they know how. It's called being passively or actively resistive and negativistic. If a parent does not realize what is happening and does not, year by year, adjust his or her style to allow more and more appropriate responsibility, one of two things happens: there is either a tense and tearful stalemate that lasts month after month or one of the sides gives up. If the parent wins, he becomes a fairly unpleasant and guilt-dogged autocrat; if the child wins, she becomes a cosmically nervous, over-powered little monster with a very warped view of her proper place in the scheme of things. Unpleasant prospects, certainly. Stalemate is what I see most often on the faces of parents when they enter my office.

I'm convinced that many parents' strategies for giving to children the necessary power to match their growing competence often lag several years behind the child's ability. This lag is not due to stupidity, negligence or lack of caring — it is because of the combination of our deep emotional involvement and the swift passage of time when we regard our children.

Not long ago a caring, concerned mother sat down across from me and, at times tearfully, told how unbearable their home life had become in the past few months. The family was one with strong, compassionate religious views, a social conscience and humane ways of treating each other. But for some reason their nine-year-old son made each day and each issue such a struggle that these everyday happenings — chores, swimming lessons, leaving the house on time, sibling disputes, playing with neighbor children — became contentious issues. The odd fact, however, was that the child was a model student, involved, tractable and easy to get along with at school!

As we untangled that web over the next two hours, it finally came clear to me when I reflected on an instance which was a metaphor for this process of growing power. The boy came into the living room with a game. Several other people were there, adults and children, but he set the game in the middle of the floor and proceeded to play it. When others asked to join, he said, "No. I want to do this by myself!" His mother was puzzled but intuitive enough to remember this clearly. It occurred to me that his statement really said, "I want this for myself, I want a piece of the action, I want to be recognized as the capable person I am." I asked this mother to consider that as a working theory and as it turned out, we were right.

She began to structure her son's life differently and talk

to him in ways that showed respect for his abilities and needs. The weekly swimming lessons were their first opportunity. He had resisted going for several weeks and always created such a furor at the time they needed to get into the car to leave that both parents were considering physical force. I helped them to realize that the lessons were their idea in the first place, not their son's idea. The chances were very good that he hadn't wanted to start them at all, but went along for a few weeks being nice about it until he felt enough frustration and resentment to act out. His parents sat down and discussed the future of the lessons. They told me that first, they apologized for not asking him whether he even wanted to take swimming, that they felt they had made a mistake. They also made a list of activities, their cost and time commitment, that their son would be interested in and planned which he would do. Swimming was simply dropped for the time being.

Later, they approached household chores in a similar way. Changes were negotiated and consequences for nonperformance were made clear. The parents told me they began to rely heavily on the use of "I - messages" (Chapter III): "I feel sad when you don't feed the dog because I know he depends on us," instead of blaming and demeaning statements such as, "Apparently you don't care if the dog starves or not." They began to transfer power and responsibilities and their appropriate consequences onto their child.

I got a call from mother about three weeks after our meeting. She said that there was a day and night difference in the level of arguing and resistance in that relatively short time. Everyone seemed to be winning. Their son began to receive the same sense of worth and ownership at home that he experienced at school with an equally caring teacher.

RESPECT

We know that respect works in a reciprocal way but there are times when I am aware that, in this society at least, it may be easy to underestimate the worth of children. The millions of children living in situations with inadequate food, medical care and child care are symptoms of our devaluing of children. The marked increase in cases of abuse and neglect speak to it vividly. Perhaps these messages sink in after a time. I don't know. I do know that underestimating children's worth and abilities is something we can't afford to do much longer, on a societal scale or in our homes.

There has been a change in the way I talk to children over the last ten years. My words and my manner have become more respectful and less intrusive. Instead of telling so much, I will ask permission to help them. Instead of lecturing, I will comment or ask a question. Instead of assuming I know what is going on within the child, I take the time to listen and observe closely and then make a tentative guess. This has come about naturally because of my growing and fundamental respect for children's resiliency, will-to-health, competence and wisdom. They are wise even though they have only been on earth for a short time and go about solving problems with the only tools they have, those we have given them.

The respect given to them is always reciprocated, although at first it so shocks some of them to be treated this way that they continue for a time to try to play the same games with me that they do with parents. After these attempts die for lack of second player, we get on with the business of changing, which is exciting. When this happens, children will listen to me because of the trust that the respect brings with it.

Another aspect of children's growth that we may not be aware of and respect is the level of sophisticated input they receive from television and from watching us try to process what happens in this increasingly complex and often chaotic world. Those struggles are not lost on them. As they become more aware that they, as children and as citizens, have certain rights, that in this world today "right" answers or "the way" to do things just aren't available anymore (as it seemed in the 1950's when I grew up), children may be saying to themselves, "Well, since we are all struggling to get by in this world together and the 'answers' are either nonexistent or ambivalent, I'd better have a say in this myself." Forgive my flirting with hyperbole here, but the point is that we must respect the fact that children are growing up with less societal, familial and cultural stability than did their parents. That has to affect the way children today respond.

YOUR CHILD IS NOT YOU

Children are, in a physical sense, extensions of ourselves as parents. However, some parents get this fact confused with the reality of a child's separateness. As good and loving a parent as they may be, they pay lip-service to the child as a separate, worthwhile-just-as-she-is person, but when their deeper values are tapped — can she go to school looking drab, unkempt or silly in something she chose that you hate? — they circle the wagons and act as if their daughter were themselves.

It is hard to grit your teeth and let the child go out the door, knowing what other parents will think of you, but that is what has to be done. You must decide whether you want to be, in Don Dinkmeyers' terms (*Systematic Training for Effective Parenting*), a "good" parent or a "responsible" parent. "Good" ones always take too much of the power in any situation involving their child; "responsible" ones always ask themselves what needs to be done that will most effectively teach their child how the real world operates. They switch off the social antenna that makes them worry about what others think. Most parents have been highly socialized to do the right thing, to say the right thing, to always be aware of our effect on others, etc., which isn't all bad, of course. Societies have to have some control and stability. But these do's and dont's we have so completely internalized often get in the way of our decision-making around issues that demand more objectivity than reflex. Your child is not you. You wouldn't relinquish the raising of your children to neighbors, would you? Then why should you relinquish those critical decisions, which make or break a child's sense of competence, to your neighbors' opinions? Their opinions may sting you a bit but you'll get over it. However, if you refuse to let your child grow by making choices and living with the consequences, you will have robbed him of something he can never retrieve.

Jim Fay, a consultant and trainer I have learned a lot from, says this: "The mistakes a child makes at five won't kill her; the ones she makes at fifteen *can* kill her." If you insist on taking most of the power to make decisions from a child over ordinary issues such as eating breakfast, clothes to wear, homework, getting along with others, and on and on, thereby stealing valuable opportunities for them to learn how, what makes you think that when your child is fourteen (or twenty) that she will automatically know how? Decision-making is not innate behavior in humans, apparently. It has to be practiced from an early age, each stage of growth encompassing more complex and serious decisions, until a child emerges with a strong, internalized set of guidelines she may draw upon when you are no longer around. Foster Cline, a child psychiatrist, says that if a child has grown up hearing only voices from outside telling her what to do, she will simply listen to a new set of outside voices when the time comes that she is no longer in the parents' twenty-four hour control. (That happens fairly soon in a child's life.)

Whose voices does she replace Mom's and Dad's with? Peers. When decisions about drugs, sex, automobiles or illegal activity surface in her life, you had better hope she has a lot of practice and experience that has taught her two profoundly simple lessons: "Good decisions make me feel good" and "Bad decisions make me feel bad." When I hurt from the inside out, as Fay says, I am bound to learn. But if I am shielded by an overprotective parent or am always punished (hurt from the outside in), there is no way for me to internalize that truth. And if I am sixteen, my lessons will be very expensive, for me and perhaps for those around me. Lessons at five or seven or nine are cheap in comparison.

WHAT DO I DO?

Your child is going to exercise his power in one of two ways: 1) he will use it to learn and grow, finding out how the world works, how he fits into it, what his strengths are, who he is, what he wants, or 2) if you deprive him of opportunities to do this legitimately, he will use it to engage you in struggles over that power. You have the choice of which one of these ways you would like him to use his power because you are older and wiser and you have set up the rules of the game in the first place. You can examine every aspect of your life with your child and decide where and how to create those opportunities for him to learn about the world and use his power to learn about himself. The marvelous side-effect is that you get the deep satisfaction that you are doing the best thing for your child's future. You no longer need to be nagged by your conscience when your child is resisting and you know something is wrong but you can't figure out what.

GUILT

If there is a common thread running through the discussions I have had with all kinds of parents — those with smoothly running (at the time) operations and those in pain (at the time) — it is a nagging sense that they haven't quite done it right, that somehow, even with children who are doing fine, they could have done this or that better or differently and so have made life a bit easier or happier for their children. I know no parents who do not admit to this! You might consider the following: you have loved, cared and nurtured, you have done the best you knew how at the time. YOUR CHILD WILL GROW UP OKAY! The chances are very slim that he will become a murderer, racketeer, thief or chronic liar. He'll be more or less confused, just as you are, more or less scared and intimidated by some things, just as you are, more or less happy, just as you are. The kids will make it even if you don't take a parenting class or change a lot. The more you worry about being a "bad" parent or dwell on your mistakes, the less energy and intelligence you will have to apply to the real joys of loving your child, watching her grow, looking for places to help her learn by making decisions. You can relax about the process because you have already laid the groundwork well. What you can do now is give her an extra little boost by your modeling of how an adult solves problems (in a calm, reasonable and optimistic way) and by allowing her proper share of power over those things in her life that will teach her the lessons of life most efficiently, without destroying her self-esteem.

There is no family without conflict and problems. There is no perfect, all-loving, all-accepting parent or step-parent. There is no right way to raise children. There is also no one who knows your child better than you do. There is no one who can do a better job than you can do if you will step back, look realistically and objectively at your child and you and make some decisions about what sort of adult you want to see them become.

CHAPTER II: STAYING COOL

If there is one thing you must begin to do right now, it is to learn how to keep your cool when your children push your buttons.

"I never get to go anywhere. You never let me do anything."

"You're mean. I hate you."

"Everybody else gets one. You're just selfish."

Did you ever hear things like that? What are these small people after, anyway? They want your heart and soul, wrapped and delivered to them, in person. The basic game of childhood is: *Get As Much As You Can* — love, candy, attention, privileges, money, you name it. That's not a lot different from most adults, but the trouble is they have a natural advantage over you as an adult. Children are first of all survivors — their instinct to survive is as strong as ours but is more "primitive" in that they go after what they see as their survival needs in a more direct, less intellectualized, socialized way. Do you recall how three year olds play? If Bobby wants the fire engine that Eugene is playing with, it seems perfectly logical and correct to Bobby to smack Eugene and take the truck. No remorse, either! As children grow, they do become a bit more sophisticated about the rules society makes about how you get what you want, but the age of children we are discussing in this book (5 - 12) are still pretty direct and they realize something you may have forgotten — that they have been dependent *for their very lives* upon you. That fact has been internalized and while it may not be literally true anymore, it still *feels like it* to that seven year old. So, if you, the "life giver" are so important, then you will be the main target of the child's strategies for survival, to "get as much as he can." You nurtured this child from birth (before, if you're the mother) and you care so much that you have lost sight of the fact that you have a master manipulator on your hands. He absorbs your moods and weak spots and he has been doing it since conception. He is more aware of your whims and needs and cares than you are sometimes. And he will use that information, not because he is vicious or mean or crazy. He is just playing the basic game.

So you need some extra protection and this is called *perspective*. There is no way you can solve a problem or help a child solve his if you are feeling angry, resentful or guilty. There are some effective ways for you to keep cool that will enable you to talk to your child so both of you can grow and learn.

What would happen to you at work if you reacted to a verbal attack or hassle in the same way you may often react to a child's bid for attention or power — yelling or demeaning or manipulating? You would probably be fired if you reacted in those ways for any length of time. What you do at work by remaining fairly calm, talking it over, and finding alternatives is what you can do at home. There is more at stake at home, I think. The rest of this chapter is devoted to perspective and practical ideas that will help you to keep your cool.

CHILDREN SEE, CHILDREN DO

Children learn most of what they know through *modeling* our behavior; they see what we as parents *do* and they copy it. They become what we *are*, not necessarily what we tell them to be. I'll explain:

From birth, children must be masters of nonverbal communication to survive. Facial expressions, cries, goos, gurgles, all body language and touch are crucial for the infant's survival. They are also impossible to fool about how we really feel about them or about ourselves. It doesn't change drastically by the time a child reaches six or seven because they're still absorbing from us our feelings and now they have sophisticated verbal skills and are well on the way to thinking as an adult thinks. But you must realize that the world operates mainly on the basis of implicit messages, or as some call them, covert messages. There is one of these buried in everything we say and do and our children pick up these messages, without fail. And they believe the implicit message before they will believe the words that are said. For example, what is the implicit message in this: "Billy, don't forget your jacket. Do you have your homework? Don't forget you have to go right to the babysitter's after school."

As well-meaning as it sounds, if this pattern is repeated day after day the clear, implicit message to the child is, "I worry that you can't handle these little things by yourself. You're really not very capable." That may be hard for you to swallow but it's all too true, I'm afraid.

Dr. Cline says, "Irresponsible children almost always are raised by loving, caring parents." If you think about it, when a parent is modeling "worry" that children won't grow up correctly and become involved in stealing power from them, what else can the child do but become "worrisome" and just the way the parent implicitly tells him to be? It's quite a setup, isn't it? A parent who models the opposite and gives underlying messages of worth and power will be showing a child "I know how to take care of myself. Therefore, so will you." This parent's messages will be full of confidence and hope and the child internalizes those instead of impotence and failure. With Billy leaving the house in the morning, a responsible parent might say, "Got everything, pal? Have a nice day. See you tonight!" The implicit message is that Billy can handle his responsibilities today and Dad has enough to handle today himself and doesn't need to worry about him, too.

Carried through a family's daily life, these messages create resilient and resourceful young people who can handle responsibility well. If Billy does forget his homework, he'll have to deal with the consequences from his teacher. If he forgets his jacket, he'll get cold. If he forgets to go to the babysitter, he may have a long way to walk back when he finds the door locked. None of which will kill him, all of which will teach him far more effectively than any of our hovering or "I told you so's."

Each time I teach a class in parenting skills, I hear this complaint: "But that's what parents are for — to make sure kids grow up right and do the right thing. I'm not willing to give up those loving reminders. It's my job." It is often a person whose own parents did the same thing and who has very little life of his or her own, even though they may be very busy and successful. They have a hard time trusting the innate competence of their children, perhaps because they don't trust their own abilities. When they stay in the class long enough, most of them usually realize how much they've been stealing from their children and they change it.

Just recently the mother of a second grader asked me to help her find the reasons for her son's persistent, loud struggles over chores, sharing with his brother and his negative school behavior. As is often the case, she looked and sounded as if she were at the end of her tether. She was, she admitted, and we unearthed the depth of her over-involvment in her child's daily life. *Mom* (she felt) had to remind, cajole and lecture about homework; *Mom* had to make sure that he had his scout uniform properly put on; *Mom* had to supervise and nag the morning routine. Or so she thought! She was just about out of gas. It's wonderful how good a motivator desperation is!

We spent the next hour exploring why she felt she must take responsibility for so much of her son's life, a life that was rightfully his to deal with. What needed to happen was: 1) the *emotional tone* of every interaction needed to be lowered considerably; 2) her *verbal output* needed to be cut at least in half; 3) she needed to decide which aspects of her son's life were *strictly his business* and then let him decide what to do about them.

How did she do this? She said, during our planning session, "I didn't think there was any way out of this!" and by the end went home with a working plan much like the one you see here:

LOWERING THE EMOTIONAL TONE

Consider what a child learns about how to solve problems when you are modeling hysterics, anger, inconsistency or irrationality. You guessed it: "This is the way adults deal with problems." How will your child respond to problems with others or difficult personal decisions? Right. The same way you do.

I can see you cringing but don't feel bad — we *all* do it from time to time. If *most* of the time you are able to remain in the adult state, reasonably calm and can "put the struggle back into the head of the child" as Fay says, then your son or daughter will be learning some profoundly valuable life-lessons: first, how to solve a problem in an effective, humane way and second, how to take control of his own life and feel the justifiable pride in doing that.

The other benefit for you, of course, is that *you* feel better — less tense, less worried and with the realization that you are truly doing the best thing for your child's long-range development. If you believe that you are "teaching" a child to be responsible by over-involving yourself in his or her business, by nagging, reminding, shielding from pain, you're mistaken. You are only fanning the fires of his discontent because he resents your being "in his face." He knows that he is capable and intelligent and your hovering says the opposite. A normal kid will resist that. And when you step back, calm down and allow the consequences of his decisions to teach him, you are then truly doing what a parent is supposed to do: prepare the child for life on his own. I can't think of anything more satisfying. Immersing yourself in the daily trivia of his life is not teaching responsibility. It is doing the opposite.

REMAINING AN ADULT

In the 1970's Transactional Analysis (Dr. Eric Berne and others) taught me some useful concepts about why things go haywire in personal interactions at times, and some of this may be useful to you in staying cool. T. A. described the three ego states that we can choose from as:

P = Parent,
A = Adult and
C = Child

P is the nurturing, sometimes authoritative or authoritarian part of us that teaches or cajoles, or lectures or takes care of others. **A** is the rational, problem-solving, working and emotionally stable part of us which accomplishes tasks and sees the world pretty much as it is.   C is the playful, creative, demanding or perhaps petulant part of us that does things like recreate, create, make love, dance, pout, or sing.

The point is, you need to stay in **A** when you are being besieged by a power-hungry or nasty **C** you live with. They would like nothing better than to "hook" *your* **C**, and you would argue with them, trade insults or threats, or get hysterical.   Your kid wins if he is able to hook your **C**. Sometimes he wants to hook your **P**, in which case you shake your finger, moralize, lecture or get your blood pressure up.   If he can't hook your **C** or **P**, he has no alternative but to deal with your **A** or give up and go away.   (I see you, you are rubbing your hands and saying "Yes, Yes!")   If you stay in **A**, you can often hook his **A** and then he is on his way to learning a lot.

Mom or Dad	Kid	

P ← ...   P   -----Tries that fail

A ——————→ A

C — — — — — —➤ C   —— Try that works

Here is what it might sound like after your child tries to hook your P or C and fails.

Kid: "I want to stay up and see the special, till 9:00."

Dad: "I'll bet you would.   Tomorrow is a school day."

Kid: "I'm going to!"

Dad: "I know you really want to see that.   Your bedtime on school night is   8 o'clock."

Kid: "I'm staying up. I don't care what you say!"

Dad: "Your bedtime has already been decided. Would you like a story tonight?"

Kid: "You never let me do anything! All the other kids can stay up. I don't like you. You're selfish."

Dad: "Well, maybe so. Story-time is in five minutes. I'll be in to read if you're ready." (Dad leaves)

Now, what happens, you may be asking, if the child refuses and sits tight? Here's what I do:

Dad: "Well, bedtime pal. Let's go."

Kid: "No."

Dad: "Tell you what: You can walk to bed or I'll be glad to carry you."

Kid: "I'm not going."

Dad: "Why don't I count to ten and when I'm done you'll have decided how you want to go." (counts to ten)

Dad: "Okay, my friend. I can see you've decided on a free trip." (Moves toward child to pick him up.)

Usually children don't choose the transportation option, mostly out of pride and the instinct to "do it myself." I have also done this with quite angry, out of control children in school settings and it nearly always works. I've only carried two children to the time-out room in the past ten years.

Why does this approach work? Because it keeps the child's *dignity* intact and lets them have at least some power of *choice* until the very end. They also are unable to blame me because I insist on remaining pleasant and reasonable.

USELESS THOUGHTS AND HELPFUL THOUGHTS

Remaining in an adult state of mind is not easy. You are going to be swimmimg upstream against the current of your own deep-seated patterns of *behavior* and *thinking*. You came from a family in which these patterns developed when you were young and therefore malleable; don't expect overnight success in changing these patterns because they have been "you" for a long time. But change they will!

The first step in changing your patterned reactions is *awareness* that they are patterns. Have you ever said something to your children and then thought, "Good heavens, that sounded just like my father!"? It's called operating "out of your gut" and it simply means that you are repeating the patterns you grew up with. Simply acknowledging that will help you change.

When you are under pressure from work, school, spouse, or child, your first instinct will be to react in your patterned way. It doesn't take any conscious thought at all, does it? You just do it. And it frequently gets you into hotter water or it doesn't help, I suspect. So, the next step after being aware that you react in set ways is to begin to consciously override the thoughts that prompt your set reactions. What I've just said probably sounds contradictory to you but it isn't and I'll give you the reasons why.

The fact is that you are operating on some very basic assumptions about yourself and the world that become "thoughts" about these things: how it should be, what kind of person you are, how other people should act, what is fair, what is not fair, and so on. For example, most of us grew up with this assumption/thought: "Children should always do what adults say." That's how I was raised anyhow. And it has caused me some problems. Why? Because if I really believe that, I will attempt to do something that is bad for both the child and me — I will try to always control that child and *make* him do what *I* want. That is not how I keep my cool and teach a child about the demands of this world.

I have chosen what I believe are five of the most troublesome thoughts or assumptions that parents accept, often unconsciously, and have countered each one with a thought which will be far more helpful in your work in trying to stay cool when things get hot. I suggest that you memorize the helpful thoughts as a way to program yourself differently. After enough time has passed and you have practiced new behavior successfully, these new assumptions will take the place of the old useless ones:

Useless Thought: Children should always do what adults say.
HELPFUL THOUGHT: Children have their own agendas and ideas. I will learn to manage children's behavior.

Useless Thought: I have to be calm and in control 100% of the time.
HELPFUL THOUGHT: It's not possible to be in control and calm all the time. I'll shoot for 80% to begin with.

Useless Thought: Children misbehave because they're being bad.
HELPFUL THOUGHT: Children are actually doing the best they know how most of the time.

Useless Thought: I can't stand it when my children are mean and rude.

HELPFUL THOUGHT: I can handle behavior problems as an adult.

Useless Thought: I must monitor and direct most aspects of my child's life.

HELPFUL THOUGHT: I will let the child direct himself in those areas that are his and I will take care of myself in my areas.

MANAGING YOUR MOUTH

You need to create "space" between the child's provocation and your reaction to it. In that space something happens that allows more objectivity and rationality in your words, more compassion in your tone of voice and facial expression, and more pride in your ability to talk, listen and guide a small person on the path to responsible adulthood. Gradually replacing your useless thoughts with more helpful ones is a good way to create the space. Now, the harder part: how do you manage to keep your mouth shut long enough?

The following list is a summary of actions you can take. It is a framework and a reminder of ideas that will be given more detail as we proceed:

1. *Stay in the adult state.* Be a "broken record" if you have to (i.e., keep repeating what needs to be done over and over).

2. *Don't get trapped in trivia.* Ignore "whose fault", "you never...", "you're wrong", etc.

3. *Recognize the feelings* that provide the fuel for the fire before you speak.

4. *Let the consequences* of the child's decision *be the teacher* of the lesson, insofar as possible.

5. *Be consistent, be consistent, be consistent, be consistent.*

6. *Allow the child to feel her own power* as you help her to solve her problems.

Here is a dialogue that may help you begin to see how this works:

Child: "Monica always is teasing me now and she won't play with me anymore. I don't want to go to school!"

Mom: "You're really upset about this, aren't you?"

Child: "She always used to play with me and now she just plays with Sarah and won't even talk to me, I hate her."

Mom: "Boy, you're angry at her."

Kid: "I hate both of them and I'm not going to school!"

Mom: "Gosh, it sounds like you'll have a pretty sad day today at school."

Kid: "I'm not going."

Mom: "Well, I guess that's not a solution to your problem. Can you think of something that might work?"

Kid: "No!"

Mom: "Not one thing, eh?"

Kid: "I could just tell them I hate them and get other girls to be mean to them."

Mom: "I suppose you could. What would happen then?"

Kid: "It would make Monica and Sarah mad!"

Mom: "Would that help you be friends again?"

Kid: "No, but I don't care."

Mom: "Maybe. Do you want to be friends with Sarah again?"

Kid: "I guess so."

Mom: "What do you think would work, then?"

Kid: "I don't know."

Mom: "You know, honey, I was a kid once and I had the same problem!"

Kid: "You did?"

Mom: "Uh, huh. Would you like to hear what I did?"

Kid: "Yeah!"

Mom: "I finally just got my friend alone, when she was in a good mood and told her how sad I was that we didn't play together any more and that I'd like it if we could be friends."

Kid: "You did? Did she stop being mean?"

Mom: "Yes, she did, but we were never best friends again though."

Kid: "Oh."

Mom: "What do you think you're going to do?"

Kid: "I guess I could talk to her."

Mom: "You're a smart and brave girl, Julie. Will you let me know what happened when you come home this afternoon? Good luck. Here comes the bus!"

A good many things happened here, didn't they? If we made a chart of what Mom *did* and *did not* do, it would look like this:

Mom Did
- Remain in the adult state
- Listen very well
- Recognize the feelings behind the issue
- Help Julie think more clearly
- Ask permission to offer suggestions
- Boost her self-esteem and confidence

Mom Did Not
- Lecture, moralize, preach, or give advice
- Try to solve the problem for Julie
- Discount or ignore the problem
- Become hooked by Julie's anger

I realize that you are often so busy and tired that you

don't have time to dialogue like this. And yet, try reading this over again aloud. How long does it take? A minute or two? Do you have the time — one or two minutes — to connect with your daughter about a crucial issue for her? Do you have the time to teach her that she's bright and capable enough to handle a hard problem? Do you have 120 seconds to let your child know that not only do you care, by listening to her, but also that you trust her to handle her social life?

All of that goes on in a two-minute exchange. If it is repeated periodically, in increasingly sophisticated ways as the child gets older, the net effect is really priceless for the child's confidence in herself and a guarantee of ongoing respect and open communication for mother and daughter.

RECOGNIZING WHY KIDS ACT THE WAY THEY DO

Other concepts which will allow you to remain more objective about you child's behavior, and thus more reasonable, come from the theories and practices of two psychologists who have had, perhaps, the greatest influence on child educators and counselors of any I know: Alfred Adler and Rudolf Dreikurs. What they have to say about misbehavior is very helpful and I'll simplify it here for you for the sake of time and usefulness. Enter it into your plans for staying cool:

1. *Behavior has a goal and a purpose.* "What is he doing now?"

You may say "So what? Everyone know that." But to internalize it when analyzing children's behavior takes some time and effort. You don't need to scratch the surface of any misbehavior very deeply to find out why the child is acting the way he is. However, you'll need to drop some of your own cherished misconceptions about the reasons for a child's behavior and replace them with an open-minded approach that concentrates on what the child is doing here and now and just as important, how other people react to what the child does. Those are the clues to what the child is after.

2. *People strive to create meaning in their lives and that provides the motivation for much of their behavior.* "Where is this leading?"

A misbehaving child may want and need to be "known" as the "bad kid" — in the absence of other options he may view as closed to him, being "bad" seems a natural way to be in this world. How and why children conceive of their own goal and ideals is personal and idiosyncratic — that is, we often can't say why in heaven's name, for sure, he decided on a goal or way of acting. But we *can see the direction* he is moving in with his behavior. What you must be on the look out for are patterns. If you boiled my usefulness as a consultant down to a specific function it is that of pattern - spotter. You can begin to spot the forest as well as the trees.

3. *Behavior is socially meaningful.* "What does he want from us?"

All of us, children, especially, are conscious of and motivated by our place in families and institutions. There will always be some clue in regard to how and why a child's behavior or misbehavior is connected to what he wants from his family, friends or school, or what he wants to be in their eyes.

4. *Belonging is a basic need.* "Where does he really belong?"

Again, a truism, yet how often even child educators ignore this simple concept! If you feel you are not acceptable you will be fearful and anxious. If you are fearful and anxious, please tell me how you will behave — calmly, reasonably and successfully or nervously, irrationally and ineptly? No one performs well who is afraid and unsure of their place in the scheme of things around them. Especially a small person who has only been on earth for six or seven years.

5. *Discouraged people act in unsuccessful ways.* "How does he see himself?"

They say, to you or to themselves, "I can't," or "It's not worth it," or "If I succeed, they'll just expect more," or "I won't." The only way I know to change behavior is to first change the attitudes, beliefs, concepts, and expectations that the person is operating from. We will work to change specific behaviors, actions which will then change our opinion of ourselves. Then we are on our way to reversing a failure cycle and creating a success cycle:

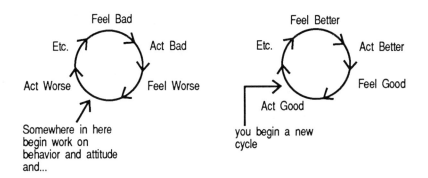

6. We are more interested in what a person decides to do with what she has than with what she has. "What will happen if he does that?"

What does she believe? Why did she do that? What is she interested in? All are questions we ask when our kids act up. Why? Because behavior is more *creative* than it is merely a *reaction* to things. Neither you nor I can accurately predict what a child will do many times because they have the capacity to *decide* what to do. But there, my friend, is where we "have" them, so to speak: once we recognize and accept this fact, we can use her *power to choose* as long as we are willing to let the consequences of a child's acts be the teachers and molders of her own behavior.

Let's move on to the second tool you must have to keep your cool.

CUTTING YOUR VERBAL PRODUCTION IN HALF

Tell me what is cheaper than *words* in most families. There is an inverse relationship between the amount you talk *at* (not *with*) your kids and the success you have in getting them to do what's necessary: the more you talk, the less they perform. Words fly forth from your lips and are lost, trampled upon, sometimes heeded, sometimes trapped and returned to you in ugly, unrecognizable forms, or most often just allowed to enter the Useless Words Zone somewhere. I mentioned earlier that most of what you will effectively teach is done through *modeling* and by the *implicit* messages buried in your surface words, your actions and body language. If you accept this fact, then you realize the truth of the old aphorism "Action Speaks Louder Than Words" and you'll become a real pragmatist in regards to your kids' behavior. And if you succeed in halving your verbal output, you find, happily, that when you very badly need to be heard, you'll probably be listened to. The older the child the more that option needs to be open. If you are currently parenting teenagers, as I am, then you realize that they are now temporarily insane and when it's time for serious talk, you want their attention.

Of course, most of what was discussed in "Lowering the Emotional Tone," will apply to helping you talk less but here are just a few more tricks to help you.

A. Make Strange Noises

I'm not suggesting squeaks and groans here, although sometimes I do feel like screaming. That doesn't work often enough I'm afraid. Try saying "Hmm" or "uh, huh" or "Gee" or "Gosh" with the proper ascending or descending voice inflection when a child rushes up to you and barrages you with his problem. Most parents' first instinct is to either ask "Why?" which is absolutely useless most of the time (they don't usually know why) or to start suggesting, lecturing or otherwise interfering where they have no business.

Years ago I learned a delightful trick by accident. It was during the dreaded noon-recess duty in a very tough school and a child raced up to me, grabbed my leg and poured out his last few disastrous and depressing minutes on the jungle gym. I was tired and preoccupied with something else and I just looked pleasantly at him and said, "Hmm" and "Gosh, I bet you didn't like that." He said, "Yeah," smiled and left, running back to the pit of disaster. I was a little shocked. I had said nothing, I thought, of value. I had not "helped." The kid was *happy* for heaven's sake! What was the world coming to if the *counselor* doesn't help?

Then I thought I'd just try it again to prove it was a fluke. They really did need me to "solve their problems." They didn't. I found that saying only, "Hmm" or "Boy!" was enough. What did they want then? Only affirmation that they hurt or were discounted or cheated, someone to sympathize with them and acknowledge that, yes, they are important. After that noon recess became more enjoyable; I could walk, watch, chat with kids and my stress level dropped. When a real conflict arose that needed a facilitator, I began to practice what I'm preaching to you here. I would listen, paraphrase, ask permission to suggest, make sure each child had a chance to be heard, and then allow them to choose a solution. (Sometimes the other choice was a trip to detention, but there always has to be a bottom line.) Anyway, it was a valuable lesson. Imagine what would happen to my cardiovascular system if, in my present school of 800 children I became hysterical over trivia, tried to impose solutions, got trapped in power struggles, spent my days in heavy Parent or in my Child: lingering, unpleasant hypertension, ulcers and, worst of all, a burned-out, negative example of a kid-hater. Once you learn to let go a little and see the results, you have to begin to rethink you own patterns of response. Hmm!

B. *Avoid Power Struggles by Imitating a Very Slow Adult*

It could be that we're blessed with too active and bountiful a brain full of ideas and opinions. It might be easier to teach children and keep healthy if that action were a little slower. When the power struggle button is pushed what you don't need is five ideas and a big mouth! The concept here is the same as was taught to my friend, a county policeman: move into a situation with appropriate force and if a look will accomplish the task, why use a nightstick? If a word will do, why pull your gun? The least intrusive method will be the most thought-provoking for the child. That is what you are after. Try these steps when you recognize a bid for a serious power contest (notice some of the same steps as before):

1. *Remember what the child is "saying" on the feeling level.* Accept it (even if you don't like it), consider that it is true for him or her (even if it seems trivial), and respond in an open way, one that does not discount the child's feelings or close off communication. Later in this book, we will discuss in detail how to do this. Is he angry, sad, discouraged? Be aware of it and acknowledge it as okay.

2. *Remain in the Adult Ego State.* As was said before, you will make the problem more complicated if you are just as irrational as your child is in a power struggle. What's worse, you'll lose. You want respect and you want to teach a valuable lesson; you will need to have your wits about you to accomplish that.

3. *Refuse to be Trapped in the Details.* Don't be hooked into arguing over whether you are mean or unfair or "he did it first" or the merits of other parents who "let" their children do things. That is all *content*; the *process* — trying to win a power struggle — is what the child really wants to succeed in. The content is a smoke-screen designed to confuse you and take advantage of you. If you will remember what *you* want, concentrate on talking as little as possible, and refuse to be moved by the gory details, you'll then be able to ...

4. *Force the Child To Think About What To Do.* Think about it: why did she come to you with that look on her

face and that whining, accusatory tone of voice? Because she wanted *you* to take on something that belongs to *her* and it is uncomfortable or unpleasant. There are several ways to keep the child focused on the fact that it is her problem and you won't get trapped in a tug-of-war with her.

Way # 1: simply remove the child from the situation. If you have exhausted your supply of listening patience and your stock of reasonable words and she still won't stop arguing about what kinds of cereal she *must* have at breakfast, you can insist that she leave until she can be more reasonable. I know many parents who just leave themselves after they have tried to be a help. Just make sure your leaving is not a way of avoiding dealing with something that needs attention.

Way #2: repeat yourself as many times as you have to until the message sinks in: Dad isn't moving on this one. I think this is also an effective form of aversion therapy — they get so sick of hearing you repeating what they don't want to hear, they just quit. Combining this with

Way #3: negative assertion, can be devastating to the young and power-mad person you are living with. I learned this from Jim Fay (*Parenting With Love and Logic*) and it works very well. What you do is accept or agree with outrageous, stupid or manipulative assertions by your child.

Child: "You're selfish!"

Dad: "I may be, but you'll need to dump the trash before you watch T.V."

Child: "I hate you!"

Dad: "I'm sorry but you'll have to dump the trash before you watch T.V."

Child: "You're probably the meanest parents on this block."

Dad: "That's possible but you'll have to dump the trash before you watch T.V."

Child: "You make me so mad. There is probably something wrong with you!"

Dad: "Could be but you'll have to dump the trash before you watch T.V."

You might be wondering, "If the kid does his job, don't you win the struggle?" Not really. You did not initiate the struggle, you have nothing to gain by his doing his job (except satisfaction), and you have no negative emotional stake in it — only his well-being in the long and short run. So you can't say that you "won." You were only doing your job.

There is one more thing you can do, however, and that's to put a positive ending on what certainly hasn't been positive enough for your child.

5. *Boost the Child's Self-Image a Little.* After an emotional situation (his) has been resolved with your refusal to be swayed by tears or threats, you may want to find some way to soften the feeling tone a bit for him, such as:

"Well, I do still like you anyway."
"You can handle this okay, I think."

"Listen, after that's done come and see me, will you?"

If you can think of nothing to say, that's all right. You haven't torn up any self-esteem and your method of staying calm and using brief neutral, consistent language has not demeaned or threatened your child. Just keep in mind that if there is something positive to end up with, the pouting period might be shorter.

By now, if you have been able to practice some of the ideas for lowering the emotional tone and for cutting your verbal production in half, you may have noticed that implementing the final recommendation for staying cool almost takes care of itself.

DECIDING WHO OWNS WHAT PROBLEM

How can you tell if it's *your* problem and not your child's?

• Your face is red. You are not smiling.
• Something or someone is interfering with your life in some small or large way.
• It's your job to manage or do something that involves your child's cooperation.

When it is your problem, remember that you are always teaching by modeling how you handle your problems. A good example is doing chores: first, whose problem is it if the child doesn't do the chores on time, at all, or incompletely? Hers? Yours? Ask yourself this question: If she *never* did the chores (and no consequences followed) would she get along just fine? The answer is , of course, yes, she would. It would not be a problem for her never to do the chores. She is smiling. You are not. Whose problem? Yours! So, here is a way to go about solving your problem:

Mom: "Christie, I notice that the garbage wasn't dumped yesterday. It really smelled up the house."

Christie: "Ah, Mom, I forgot. Geez, I always have to dump the trash. It's not fair."

Mom: "Well, it's something that needs to be done and this month it is your turn."

Christie: "I can't remember that every day! I'm really busy. I've got a ton of homework!"

Mom: "Since the rule is that it gets dumped daily, it is hard for me to imagine any other way. Can you?"

Christie: "Kevin could do it once in a while."

Mom: "Uh, huh. Next month."

Christie: "Gol, that's too long."

Mom: "Maybe. Tell you what: the garbage needs to be dumped daily by 5:30 p.m. If you forget, I'll wake you up early the next day so you can have time to do it before school."

Christie: "What time?"

Mom: "Oh, half-hour, 45 minutes early, so you can get ready too."

Christie: "No way!"

Mom: "Well, take your choice, honey, morning or night."

Now, mom will have to follow through if Christie forgets, in a way that doesn't cause mom much trouble. What if the early rising is not possible? There are, surely, things that go on after 5:30 p.m. that Chrisite would not want to miss, like T.V. or play time or talking on the phone to friends, aren't there? And she would miss them because you would enforce the rule about garbage dumping.

A SPECIAL WORD ABOUT HOMEWORK

I put homework in a special class of "whose problem" because it is so easily confused. More parents get this one wrong than any other child-raising issue I run into. Whose problem is homework, anyway? The way many (probably most) parents act, you would really believe that a child's homework is their problem! They worry about it, nag about it, spend endless hours either talking to the child or the teacher about it, and sometimes even *do* it for the child.

It is easy to confuse this issue because of a simple fact we know and the kid doesn't: if you don't get a good solid basic skills foundation, you are going to have trouble down the road. So, you see this ten year old, blithely strolling into the lion's den of harder and harder school work, hardly lifting a finger, not knowing what the long-term consequences are.

And, mom, dad, it isn't your problem. That's the rub!

Homework is between the child and his teacher and you do have an important job in it, but ultimately it is his to do and be responsible for the consequences. And watching him "blow it," possibly for long-range trouble, is just about impossible for most of us. Is there a way out here?

Of course. From an early school age, you will need to be: 1) doing the things suggested in this book in regards to rule enforcing and communicating, and 2) define clearly each person's role in the quicksand pit of homework.

Here are what ought to be your respective roles:

Mom and Dad's Role	Child's Role
1. Provide the place and materials. A desk, chair, good lighting, writing materials, reference books, etc.	1. Get it home. 2. Get it done. 3. Get it back.
2. Set the rules: "You may watch T.V. as soon as homework is finished," or some variation of that.	
3. Answer specific questions about a problem.	
4. Go away and do your chores.	

If you insist on going beyond those four parts of your role, you have crossed the line into your child's territory and, usually by nagging and worrying, relieve him of the burden of worrying about it. Most kids are savvy enough to let you do that.

Here is a quote, from at least twenty parents in the last year:

Me: "How long does it take to do his homework?"

Them: "Oh, I bet we spend two or three hours every night."

Good heavens! Can you imagine what is happening to your relationship with your son or daughter if you spend nearly all of your and their free time engaged in a battle over a problem that you should be involved with for, at the most, five or ten minutes? The parents quoted above, when they came to see me, were quite understandably on the edge of mayhem since their relationship had eroded so much that it was coloring every other issue in their lives in negative tones.

These parents did some simple, effective things, but the hardest for them was to *stand back and allow the child to fail* if that's what the child chose to do. Once they accepted the fact that you really can't *make* anybody do anything (short of murder threats) and responsibility is taught by *giving* it, things got better. The parents carry out their roles quietly, nonstridently, biting their tongues to keep quiet; the child eventually (it may take one awful report card) realizes he is on his own, the pride which resides in most children asserts itself and he begins to perform.

With homework, if a parent takes most of the power and responsibility over from the child, the parent ends up in a real losing game. Not only does the child learn a destructive lesson on how to get what he wants, but he also doesn't develop the ability to self-start when it is time to study or do a report or write an essay. Will you accompany your child to the university and come over to his dormitory room each night to remind him to do his calculus? Will you hide behind parked cars after the dance to see that no hanky-panky is going on? When will you begin to let this child own the problems that are truly his and live with the consequences of the decisions he makes around those problems? Making a dumb decision can be uncomfortable at ten; it can be deadly at seventeen.

I hope that it is evident how interrelated the three parts of the prescription for staying cool are: 1) lowering the emotional tone of interactions, 2) cutting your verbal production in half, and 3) deciding who owns the problem and letting them solve it. You will need to be working on each one simultaneously as you go about the daily business of life with your child. There are ways to talk that provide the lubrication for the mechanics of doing this and the next chapter will enable you to listen and respond effectively, especially when things get tense.

CHAPTER III: BEING HEARD

We all know what anger and frustration we feel if someone doesn't listen. You know that one of the quickest ways to make an enemy or lose a friend is to seem uncaring about what someone is saying to you. The implicit message that a poor or distracted listener gives another is "I don't care about you. What you are is not important." We don't often treat our friends in such a disdainful way because we know what they will do. Why, then, do we so often — more than is excusable by our being busy or tired — listen so badly and infrequently to our children? I think we realize that behind each thing a child says to us stands a *feeling* that we sometimes cannot or will not recognize. It may be threatening to us or it may not occur to us that there is a feeling there at all, but be assured, there is a feeling behind the words and that's where we have to start if we want our kids to listen.

HOW WE DISCOUNT KID'S FEELINGS

Starting today, be aware if you are doing any of the following:

1. Considering feelings as unimportant. "Oh, that's not so bad. You'll learn to get over people being mean to you. Come on!"

2. Denying that the feelings exist. "You do not hate your brother! How could you ever even think about such a thing! We don't hate people in this family. You're just

making something out of nothing!"

My own parents did a good job of raising my two brothers and me. Our family was close and we were able to talk to each other. But my parents were uncomfortable with my anger toward my siblings and toward them. I can't tell you why — perhaps because of the way each of my parents was raised. In any event, my hateful feelings toward others in my family were not accepted. As a youngster, I recall hearing, "You don't hate your brother," or "Don't you ever say that to your mother" when I expressed anger. My parents weren't (and aren't) strange or abusive. They were caring and thoughtful and good parents to have — but angry feelings were very scary to them. So I got an awfully confusing message as a child that went like this:

"I feel like I want to hurt him. My body is tight and my face is flushed. The words I learned for this are 'mad' and 'hate'. But Mom and Dad say that I don't have this feeling! How could this be? There must be something wrong with this feeling or with me because they know best."

I grew to adulthood being confused about what anger was, if it was ok or not ok, and how to express it. Given this, I swallowed the anger. It went "underground" — that is, it became self-pity and depression. The reason I know this is that a skilled therapist and I unearthed it after an unpleasant divorce from a marriage where neither one of us knew how to express our angry feelings in a healthy way. It has taken me years to accept the *legitimacy* of my anger and to *express it* appropriately.

You can't teach your children how to accept and express

their own feelings if *you* don't accept them as valid and normal. All our feelings come out of the same "pot" so to speak. All feelings, from deep depression or sadness to the highest ecstasy are all part of our genetic make up, and since these feelings come from the same source, they are connected to each other. If you can envision all of your feelings on a continuum such as this,

Depressed Sad Mad Grumpy Miffed Neutral Ok Good Happy Joyous Ecstatic

perhaps you can imagine what starts to happen when you do not allow yourself to feel sadness, for example. Since the source of sadness is the same wellspring of emotion that produces joy, you will find that your ability to feel and express joy will be impaired along with your squelching of sad feelings. If your suppression of your "uncomfortable" feelings goes on long enough, you will find that you can't feel and show your "comfortable" ones either and you may end up with a range of emotions that is very narrow:

Depressed Sad Mad Grumpy Miffed Neutral Ok Good Happy Joyous Ecstatic

↑

All you are left with
to acknowledge and show.

Just being neutral most of the time is handicap enough but it doesn't remain that way for a person who can't recognize and accept all of her feelings. Since these emotions are part of our genetic heritage, their power is such that the suppression of them causes more destructive behavior than merely producing a person with a flat emotional range. Those buried feelings may hurt everyone concerned, or a person may become so depressed that it interferes with any normal functioning. You obviously want to know how to prevent these things from happening. But you must be aware that if you deny or discard the feelings of your children and do not allow appropriate expression of them, you run the grave risk of creating some long-term problems.

3. <u>Listening badly</u>. You may truly care and accept the child's feelings but please remember that you must *show* that by stopping, looking at the child while she is talking, and responding in ways that indicate you really are listening and caring about what she says.

Tara: "Dad?"

Dad: "What is it sweetie?" Dad puts down the paper and looks at her.

Tara: "The dog bugs me."

Dad: "What do you mean?"

Tara: "Well, he gets hair on the rug and I can't lay down on it. My clothes get all hairy."

Dad: "That's not pleasant. What do you want to do about it?"

Tara: "Well, you could vacuum every day instead of just Saturday."

Dad: "Hmm. Do you know how to vacuum?"

And so on. What you do in small ways, that take such

minute amounts of time, is so important. A child may not say to you, "I know you're not really listening because you're still occupied with something else," but they will either think it or feel it.

4. <u>Offering advice that bypasses the underlying feelings</u>.

Roger: "Those guys are still chasing me and hitting me at recess."

Dad: "Listen Roger, I'll tell you what you need to do tomorrow. Go up to those boys and tell them that they have no right to bother you and if they don't stop, you're going to have your dad call that school and get the principal down on them."

This is not the way to encourage a child to express his emotions or to solve problems by himself. A response such as the one Dad gave is actually debilitating to a child because it bypasses the hurt feelings of the child and it totally leaves him out of contributing to the solution to what is really his to solve or get help solving.

Unasked for advice is nearly always useless and unwanted; worse, it discounts why the child brought the subject up in the first place — he's hurt and worried. Those feelings come first. He wants validation of those feelings a lot more than he wants any advice. You are his home base in trying to structure his world as a safe and predictable place and your first task is that of reassurance. When you have done that — sometimes that's all they really want — then you can move on to the problem solving part. Notice I didn't say "advice."

Advice is demeaning to another person *unless it is asked*

for specifically. Unwanted advice sends to that person this simple, negative unspoken message: "Since you don't know much and can't be trusted to figure this out for yourself, it is my job to tell you how to solve this problem." There is always time and a vital need for parental advice; we are qualified (and obligated) to give it. I'm just asking you to pick the *time* and the *way* in which you offer it very carefully. If it is in the context of a problem-solving, two-way discussion and if it is offered in the spirit of possibly helping and not dictating, advice from you is valuable.

5. <u>Defending the person the child is upset with</u>. "Well, don't you ever think about how your little sister feels? She can't do things nearly so well as you and you could just ease up on her when all she wants to do is look at your model car."

6. <u>Questions that ignore the feelings</u>. "Why did he do that? What were you doing in the yard anyway? Why didn't you just tell him to stop it or you'd go home? Where is he now, anyway?"

When I am hurting in some way — sad, dejected, disappointed, left-out — the very last thing I need is for my wife or my friend or relative to give advice, start questioning me, appear distracted or bored, or worst of all, tell me what I'm going through is nonsense. What I want is for them to simply listen and understand, to show me the sort of empathy that I hope I show to them. Even saying *nothing* and a hand on my shoulder is far more effective in soothing my feelings and cementing the bond between us.

My wife and I are both counselors, she with college-age students and adults, I with children and parents. One day she came home very much discouraged about an incident at work. I said something that I'm going to suggest that you learn, but it backfired. I said:

"I'll bet you're pretty sad about that!" She said, "Cut the counselor talk b___ s___ Jon! All I want is a hug."

Enough said? With adults who are aware of their feelings and have a pretty solid view of their own abilities and processes, the suggestions you will read in this chapter may be unnecessary or useless (as in the case of my wife). But with children, whose vast experience totals seven or ten years, the ways of talking and responding you will learn are crucial in teaching them to recognize and define their feelings and in showing them how ready you are to accept *all* of them — bad feelings and good ones.

LEARNING TO RECOGNIZE AND ACKNOWLEDGE FEELINGS

You are going to learn the difference between an _Open Response_ and a _Closed Response_ and then begin to practice these responses as soon as you can. An _Open Response_ is so called because it leaves open the possibility of more talking between the two of you. The speaker sees that you are ready to accept and to listen to her thoughts and feelings.

A _Closed Response_ denies or ignores the feelings expressed and is so called because it quickly and effectively closes down the channels of communication. Here are examples of a _Closed Response_:

Ben: "Mrs. Martin is just an old bag! I wasn't even talking!"

Mom: "Now don't you talk that way about Mrs. Martin!"

Dad: "Yeah. You've got to pay to play, kiddo. Shrug it off."

Ben is guaranteed not to talk any further about the incident. And he's probably boiling inside more than before he opened his mouth. Here is how you can give and <u>Open Response</u>:

1. Describe to yourself <u>how the child is feeling</u> right now. Use <u>one word</u>.

<u>Child Says</u>	<u>Child is Feeling</u>
"Mrs. Martin is an old bag!"	Angry/Mad

2. Use that <u>one</u> feeling word in <u>one</u> sentence to respond.

<u>Child Says</u>	<u>You Say . . .</u>
"Mrs. Martin is an old bag!"	"It sounds like you're pretty mad about something."

This is the first step in an Open Response. You might really need to discuss the positive sides of Mrs. Martin or basic respect for teachers or how he got himself into the situation. But you will probably never get the chance if you stop the initial communication with a Closed Response! There is time for those discussions later.

Complete the right-hand side of the chart below with <u>one sentence</u> statements that include the word describing the feeling of the child whose statement appears at the left.

You may want to vary your responses, using phrases such as "It seems like you are _____." or "Are you feeling _____ about this?" (#1 is done for you.)

Your Child Says . . .

You Say . . .

1. "I can't figure this out. It's too hard!"

"It sounds like you're discouraged."

2. "Oh boy: School's out in ten days."

3. "All the other kids went to the beach. I don't have any-one to play with."

4. "I was mean to Timmy. I was bad I guess."

5. "Go away and leave me alone. I don't want to talk to you or anybody."

6. "I'll never play with Pamela again! She's a dope and a creep!"

7. "Do you think I'm doing this report right? Is it enough?"

8. "I'm not having any fun. I
can't think of anything to do."

_____

9. "I can do it myself. I don't
need you to help me."

_____

10 "Look Dad, I made this
airplane."

_____

11. "I'll never be good like
Jason. I practice and he's
still better."

_____

12. "It's my hair, isn't it? I
can wear it any way I want
to!"

_____

13. "William's mom and dad let
him ride *his* bike to school."

_____

14. "Mrs. Martin is just an old
bag! I wasn't the only one
talking."

_____

15. "She gives us too much homework.
I'll never get it all done."

_____

It would help you fix this pattern in your mind if you get another person to alternate reading the statements and then giving your responses out loud. Then make it a point today or tomorrow to begin to use this sort of response when a child comes to you with a feeling-loaded statement. Remember when your parents told you that "To have a friend, you must be a friend." It works that way with listening: "To be listened to, you must first be a listener."

Here are some examples that will help you get a feel of how this skill works in the real world:

Mom: "Time for dinner. Please come to the table."

John: "In here!" (meaning the T.V. room)

Mom: "Dinner's ready at the table."

John: (Sullenly entering) "The football game's on. I want to see it."

Mom: "You're pretty determined to eat and watch but you know the rules."

John: "Yeah. Why can't you just lighten up. Gol, one time!"

Mom: "Well, dinner's at the table."

John: "I hate you!"

Mom: "You may not like it but I would rather you found another way to express you anger in the future. I don't like that at all."

John: "Geez! No breaks!"

Mom: "Let's sit down. You can go back in and
watch as soon as we're finished."

The mother who reported this to me had talked with me a week or two before this conversation took place, expressing her anger over John's frequent attempts to push her buttons by using the "I hate you" routine. She is a single parent and was already feeling on the down-side of confident about providing a good home and working a fifty-hour week. She did not have to accept, without protest, deliberately hurtful statements. She did acknowledge and accept the feelings but she did not have to put up with what I consider his verbal harassment of his mother. She deserved a medal for her self-control and persistence. Here is another:

Son: "Barry is being mean to me. He won't let me play with his scooter! I'll hit him if he doesn't let me!"

Dad: "You're pretty angry at Barry."

Son: "Yeah. He's a brat. I hate him!"

Dad: "Hmm."

Son: "He'll never get to play with any of my stuff."

Dad: "I see."

Son: "He'll be sorry." (He leaves and goes back outside.)

When the father related this short exchange to me , he

was excited and pleased about what had happened because he had "done his job" with very little effort and the outcome suited everyone. The purpose — simply giving credibility to hurt feelings — was served.

His older son came up to him later with a puzzled look on his face and asked, "Dad, why are you saying 'Hmm' so much?" That brings up some precautions we need to discuss.

1. <u>Don't always repeat what a child has said in order to show your empathy.</u> It isn't necessary when a child is saying matter-of-fact kinds of statements. Use your listening and responding skills for high or negative emotions.

2. <u>Gear your responses to the intellectual and emotional sophistication of your child.</u> Just being there with a distraught teenager and nodding your head might be enough; a lot of talk, even empathetic, may be intrusive.

3. <u>Make sure that your tone of voice and body language fit the words you use.</u> A flat, bored "You seem sad." is worse than saying nothing because, as stated here before, they will read the nonverbal before the verbal if the two don't match.

4. <u>All feelings are acceptable, but the way they are expressed to you may not be.</u> As in the case of the boy who wanted to watch television and eat at the same time, a parent doesn't have to put up with verbal or physical expressions of feelings that are unacceptable to your family. It is very important that you stop that kind of inappropriate behavior. The best way I have found to do that is a firm, flat statement that it is not acceptable and should cease, i.e.-

"I know you are mad at Jimmy but you may not scream at him. If you would like to scream you may go into your room and close the door."

5. <u>Don't worry if you blow it by either guessing wrong or being tired and less than sharp in your response.</u> You are human and, best of all, you'll get another shot at it sooner that you want it!

Now we need to move on to what you say to a child when it is *your* problem. The child has said something or done something that has interfered with your life or rights in some way, or has broken a rule or misbehaved. Keep in mind what we have discussed so far: the *least* intrusive, *most* adult, dignity-saving response you can muster. And I'd like to teach you an easy, effective way to accomplish all of that: It's called an "I-Message."

Fifteen years ago when I was first beginning to shift out of my Fascist phase of handling discipline problems at school — yelling, dictating, browbeating — a little incident changed forever the way I talk to children.

A very tough young man of eleven had just made the obscene finger gesture to a girl down the hall and yelled an unpleasant remark to her. I had to talk to myself to stifle my typical, finger-pointing, blaming "how dare you" response because I was learning new ways to handle discipline; so I came out of my room, asked him to step over against the wall and saw his legs spread, chin-out "I'm ready for you, teach" defiance. Luckily, he and I had had no serious confrontations before this. I said:

"Bobby, it really makes me sad to see you treat other

kids that way. I know you somewhat and I know you're a pretty nice kid. I guess I'm just disappointed."

And I walked away. Out of the corner of my eye, I saw his face fall and his eyes widen. A neutral adult had just pulled his fuse and his patterned reaction to being chewed out by teachers was useless. There was no provocation, and you bet he thought about what I said. We got along well all year and I became a sort of base for him to touch when he was feeling scratchy and ready to start trouble.

As I realized what had happened, I began to use I-Messages and to me they seemed almost magical. Sometimes it so startled kids who expected to be lectured or demeaned, that they would simply stop what was going on that was out of line. I'm suggesting that you may find similar success with this.

HOW TO TELL CHILDREN YOU ARE NOT HAPPY

In the chart below there are several situations described and a typical blaming or demeaning "You-Message" next to it. Your task is to change the "You-Message" to an "I-Message". The easiest way to do this is to remember the 1,2,3, of I-Messages:

    1. I feel _____(name your feeling)

    2. when you _____(describe the behavior)

    3. because _____(tell why it's bothering you).

Here is an example:

Your son comes in and slams the door, takes a glass roughly out of the cabinet, gulps water, spilling some on the floor, and attempts to rush back out. You could say, "Justin, hold on there pal. Slow down. I feel angry when you are careless around the kitchen because it makes messes others have to clean up. Please wipe up after yourself. Now, please."

Now it's your turn. (You may follow the I-Message with a short command.)

Problem	You-Message	I-Message
Child procrastinates about going to bed. Mom and dad want to talk alone. Child hangs around.	"You know it's past your bedtime. You Need sleep. You're annoying us"	
Child asks repeatedly to be taken to the park. But she hasn't completed a chore that was expected to be done several days ago.	"You don't deserve any treats because you haven't cleaned your cat's litter box yet."	
Children have the radio on so loud that you can't hear or concentrate.	"Why do you have to have that so loud? Don't you ever think of anyone else in this house?"	
Child has promised to clean windows for a party that evening. He has fooled around all day and now there is an hour before people start arriving.	"You have messed around all day and you could have had this done. You really make me mad."	

Child has been pouting for about 5 hours. You don't know why.	"Stop that pouting right now. You're going to trip on your lower lip. Come on!"
Child comes to dinner with a dirty face and hands.	"Big boys don't eat with dirty hands. Go wash right now."
You want to read but your child keeps coming to you to ask questions or make minor complaints.	"You shouldn't bother me when I'm reading."
Your 16 year old son likes to take both hands off the wheel on straight stretches of road.	"You're gonna wreck doing that someday. I'm not kidding!"
Child comes in fifteen minutes late for dinner.	"How many times have we told you to get in here on time. You're holding us up."
Your child folds only her own laundry after a wash and leaves everyone else's in a pile.	"That's a pretty selfish way to act. You should think about other people here."

The "battle" to get kids to grow up right is won or lost in the trenches, that is, the daily problems, chores, hassles, discussions that go on in the life of each family. Having a way of responding to minor irritations or mistakes that children are prone to get into is crucial to your relationship and thus to your long-term goals for the child. If ten times a day your son or daughter gets a neutral I-Message instead of a blaming, self-esteem lowering You-Message, consider what the payoff will be in just six months. The reason I-Messages work is simple and powerful: you have taken responsibility for your own feelings and have said in an honest way what you want. The implicit message there is one of trust in the child and caring about how she learns about the world. Messages of this kind are too basic *not* to work!

We've learned how to listen to children in a way that will encourage further talk and convince them that you are on their side; we've practiced responding in ways that preserve a child's dignity and allow you to say what's on your mind. Now, as you have probably been wondering, what do you do to get that child *moving*! Let me quote a very practical-minded father in our last parent group:

"That's all really helpful, Jon, and it works like you say, but I still am having trouble when it's time for him to get his little *!#* in gear! What's next?"

SENDING MESSAGES OF EMPOWERMENT

I've warned you against accusing, demeaning, blaming, and dictating. To be fair to you, here are some things to replace those old habits.

1.   *Instead of talking too much, USE ONE OR TWO (MAYBE THREE) WORDS.*
Hundreds of little things that must be done to make a house and family run smoothly are all in your consciousness but they aren't in your children's. There is no sense fighting a losing battle by expecting that they will remember everything as you do, nor is it wise to decide that you can change their forgetfulness by nagging or punishing. Make

it easy on yourself by using a word or phrase at the proper time.

You're leaving the house and your daughter's bedroom light is still on: "Karin, your light."

Your son is headed out the door and his books are still on the table: "Robert. Books."

Your daughter is using your expensive watercolor paper for doodling: "Shannon, different paper." (I handed her some scrap.)

Keep in mind why you are doing this: your object is the task at hand, no big issue. Kids are kids and their minds work differently. However, you might be thinking I'm contradicting what I said earlier about letting the child find out the consequences of what she does by reminding. Here's what to remember: If you *always* must remind, then you have taken over your child's job and then must let the chips fall for him. We're talking here about a few words once in a while. The implicit message you send with just a few words is that they're bright enough to catch your drift without a lecture and responsible enough to do it.

2. *Instead of demeaning or accusing, simply GIVE THE CHILD INFORMATION SHE NEEDS AT THE TIME.*

It is difficult not to put on the manner of your own parents and refrain from moralizing and being condescending when you see things so obviously in need or correction. But remember the fallout if you succumb! Here are two examples of how it works.

Her closet is such a mess she can't find anything when she wants it: "Chrisie, when I come home I just stand right in front of my closet, get undressed and hang everything up. Then it's done in one minute. You might want to try that."

Then get out! This works for some children. In regards

to her room, I tried it with my daughter and it didn't work. After weeks of nagging (no change) and two days of threats (even worse), I realized that as long as the door was closed, I didn't really care about what condition her clothes were in. Not so strangely, when I ceased playing into a power struggle that my sweet little third grader was winning, she took better care of her room. The only information that ever did much good was when guests were coming over and I said, "Shannon, there will be a lot of people here tonight. I think they might need your room to leave their coats." You should have seen her move! A great excuse for a party!

3. *Instead of haranguing and dictating, WRITE IT DOWN.*

My son, Justin, had skipped his turn at the dishes, out of forgetfulness or distaste, I don't know which, nor did it really matter. He happened to be in a foul mood most of the time when around the house (he was in love) and I knew no matter how neutral or humane I said what I wanted, he'd create a hassle since he was at the time a victim of his own hormones. So I wrote him a letter and pinned it to the couch that sits next to the front door for him to read when he returned from his date at 11:30.

Here is what it said:

"Dear Justin:

I noticed that the dishes were sitting undone on the counter. Since you know the rule is that they're done prior to breakfast, I'll be glad to get you up when I get up tomorrow (Sunday) at 6:30 if you'd like.
Hope you had a good time tonight.
Love, Dad"

I happened to be awake, reading, when he came in and he groaned and slammed a cupboard or two but he did the dishes.

When you leave notes, be creative and have a light touch. Well-placed humor works well, too. Here's a note I left on the bathroom mirror.

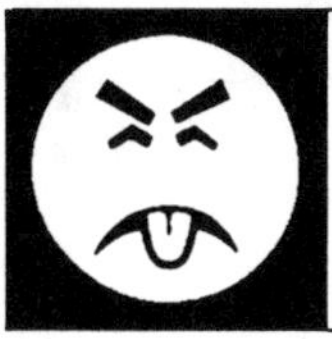

> "These toothbrushes sitting in slime are very dangerous and contain alien and ugly creatures that will cause brain damage!"

The implied messages in a written reminder, especially a good-natured one, are that these problems are routine and not worth major confrontations and that, of course, is all that your child needs to comply because he's a good kid. And when you leave notes for no particular reason, such as a surprise "I love you" note in a sack lunch or "I'm thinking of you" inside a book, then the notes of polite demand become even easier to accept.

4. *Instead of blaming, TELL HOW THEIR BEHAVIOR AFFECTS YOU.*

My oldest daughter has been known to spend over an hour on the phone — with the same person! Hard to believe, isn't it? This causes a problem because of the possibility (she obviously doesn't believe it) of someone wanting my wife or me on the phone. So again I stifle my urge to rip the phone from her hands and I say:

"Karin, when you spend so long on the phone it makes it impossible for me to receive any calls. And I have a need to talk to my friends, too, just as you do. Please hang up in one minute."

You may have noticed that this is a form of an "I-Message" that we discussed earlier in this chapter. It works for the same reasons. Another example (this was necessary when "Shannon, the dog's dish is empty," didn't work):

"When I see the dog go without food for over a day, I feel really sorry for her. I bet she's hungry and it makes me pretty sad. She depends on us to feed her since she can't do it herself."

This message combines needed information a nine year old may have forgotten as well as the effect of her neglect. It worked very well at the time.

5. *Instead of hogging all the power in an issue, ASK FOR YOUR CHILD'S HELP.*

As a school principal, I spent a lot of time (more than I wanted!) calling parents of misbehaving students for a conference to help draft a plan for change. What I found very successful with upset and angry parents I began to use also with my own children and it worked just as well. I would call and instead of beginning the conversation with: "Robbie has been misbehaving and I'd like you to come in and talk this over," I began the conversation with: "Hello, Bill. This is Jon, the principal at _____. I need your help with something."

It isn't very effective to try to solve a difficult problem when one person is in an "up" position and one is "down;" too much defensiveness usually gets in the way. Very few people can refuse a request for help, especially children.

I then started to use this approach with students. One day I called in two boys whom I knew were intimidating other students at lunch recess.

Me: "Hi, guys. I heard of a problem and I need your help solving it."

Boy 1: "What?"

Me: "Well, six kids and two teachers told me that you boys were chasing people who didn't want to be chased and you were teasing them a lot, too. That creates a real problem I think you can help me solve. Do you want to know what that problem is?"

Boy 2: "Yeah."

Me: "The problem is, when other kids see you hassling kids and making their lunch recess unhappy, they think that's ok to do here at _____School. Is it ok to do that sort of thing here?"

Boy 2: "No."

Me: "You're a smart kid; it isn't ok. But when you do it, it sure gives the other kids the wrong idea. How can you help me make sure the other kids don't get the wrong idea?"

Boy 1: "We could tell them that it's not all right."

Me: "That's true. What else would show them it's not ok?"

Boy 2: "We could say, I'm sorry."

Me: "That would be great."

Boy 1. "We could just not chase them."

Me: "You guys are brilliant. I think you've got this thing whipped. Will you come and see me tomorrow and again next week and tell me how it's working?"

Now, you're aware that these second graders were on the spot. How else can you explain the ready answers? They were nervous and did not like the fact that the boss had found out their game. But the point here is how I went about giving them the message, STOP IT. They were far more ready to stop the behavior than if I had accused and lectured. And my goals as an educator and surrogate parent were met: teach life skills, maintain or raise self-esteem, and keep everybody safe. I had raised their awareness of their misbehavior and its effect on all of us and let them verbalize what they already knew to be the right thing to do, then gave them encouragement to do it and a reminder that I was watching their progress. Most children respond well to those approaches.

You may expect a lot less cooperation and ready answering when you try this with your own children. Having the principal or teacher lower the boom is scarier than when mom or dad does it, but you've been learning ways and attitudes to help you stick to your guns and get what you want. Asking for a child's help when you need to solve a problem with her will work, too. You are, indeed, asking for and in need of their help but the form their help will take is up to you.

Mom: "Hey guys, come here. I've got a problem here in the kitchen I need your help with."

Son 1: "What's the matter?"

Mom: "I've gotten home from work the last three nights and when I came in to start supper, I see the dirty dishes on the counter, the counter's greasy, and the drawers are left open. And I'm saying to myself, how can I get dinner ready for hungry boys if I have to clean up someone else's mess?"

Son 1: "Well, just ignore it. You gotta clean up after supper again anyway."

Mom: "I guess for me that's not an option for a couple of reasons: one, preparing a meal takes a clear deck and two, I don't think it's fair for me to clean up someone else's mess."

Son 2: "Look Ma, I know you're just wanting us to clean up when we come home for lunch. Why don't you just say so?"

Mom: "I already did on Monday; this is Thursday. Nothing happened."

Son 1: "Gol, Mom, we only have a half hour at noon!"

Mom: "I'm aware of that. And I need the kitchen clean when I get home. Any ideas?"

Son 2: "Have the dog lick it up! Ha, Ha!"

Mom: "Sure."

Son 1: "We could just eat faster so we could clean up."

Mom: "That would work. Also, I was thinking that if you guys are so pressed for time, it might be better for you to go back to eating in the school cafeteria."

Son 2: "No way. I'm not eating that garbage!"

Mom: "I tell you what — let's see what happens between now and next Thursday. You help me out by cleaning up after yourselves at noon so I can start supper and I'll assume you can handle coming home to eat. If not, it's stay at school."

Son 2: "No chance."

Mom: "I guess you could skip lunch altogether if you want. OK with me. Now please clean up and I'll get the chicken on."

These two teenagers got a firm, fair, and loving message from their busy mom. She refused argument and basically told them what their choices were: cooperate, go hungry, or eat elsewhere. The parent who related this story to me had been divorced a few months before it took place and it was the first time she had been as clear and firm as this, finally realizing that her feelings of guilt and her distraction after the divorce had prevented her from doing many things that eventually would make their lives easier and teach her two boys some valuable lessons. You can bet she didn't return to her old wishy-washy methods.

The last two incident descriptions illustrate a point you have already had experience with: the approach toward children of different ages varies in the amount of "tough love" that mom or dad must give out. It takes a good deal of positive self-esteem (and some bravado, too) to stand your ground and nicely demand that children stop what they are doing and change it the way you want it. We will be discussing that aspect of your overall plans later in this book.

In this chapter, you have learned about and should now be practicing how to recognize and respond to feelings and how to send validating and empowering messages to your children. The groundwork is fairly solidly laid if you are finding even small successes each day with these approaches. You are now ready to be far more effective as a disciplinarian. The reason so many parents fail at the disciplining end of the relationship continuum is that they get the cart before the horse; that is, they expect their rules and regulations to be followed without having first spaded the fertile soil of their communication, trust, and mutual respect.

CHAPTER IV: DISCIPLINE

A few years ago I owned one of the dumbest, most affectionate golden retrievers you've ever seen. The breeders told me that one of the pups had been dropped on its head and it worried them. I got her. I think they knew it was her because I bought the dog for half price. Anyhow, training this nice but slow animal was a chore, to put it mildly; she was late being housebroken, commands were something she never really understood consistently, training her to the leash never happened and heaven knows, I tried! The obedience school instructor, after first chuckling and telling me "Never met a dog I couldn't teach to lead" finally admitted by the end of the class that I had an "unusual" dog. She was sweating and forcing a smile at the time as I recall.

But trying to get the dog to go to her box in the corner of the kitchen and to lay down drove me to distraction. It was crucial that this large, affectionate dog be out of the way when indoors and however much I tried, however many time-tested rules of dog training I invoked, she never would just go and sit or lie until called out.

"Sasha," I would say, over and over, "back in your box!"

She would look, wag her body, and come over to me, or she would wander out into the dining room. And I began after a while to have delicious fantasies of her running off, never returning and me relieved of the guilt of actually considering either selling her or having her put to sleep. But I can thank this nerve-jangling dog for making me think further about discipline and how we go about it when kids demand it.

The first thing I thought was that there aren't many retarded or severely emotionally disturbed children compared to average, doing-pretty-well kids. In a school setting the children in need of serious, on-going intervention get it at a fairly young age. That means that the average child that I see or whose parents I talk to is perfectly capable of performing competently. So why don't they? If they are *able*, and not like dear Sasha, unable, why do kids so often act as if they *can't*?

The answer to this became gradually more clear as case after case turned up in the mode of one mentioned earlier in this book — of the child who is performing very well in school and being an absolute terror or jerk everywhere else. A pouting, difficult child at the babysitters, a whining, demanding monster at home, but a reasonable, helping person in class. Those types became my most successful cases for a simple reason that it didn't take mom and I very long to understand: the child, being normal and bright enough, learned "Stay in your box!" at school and did not learn it at home. After running the power struggle, manipulation, pout-till-you-get-your-way routine past his teacher, the child was either ignored or suffered the consequences of the behavior enough that s/he stopped it at school. But home, sweet home — a place still to stomp and rage and push adults around, what joy! Once the parents realized what was happening and that the child was indeed able to maintain at school, most cases like this showed progress in as little as two weeks — if the parents went to work and followed through!

This is how we start our discussion about changing the way parents discipline: I draw a box like this:

and tell the parents, "Your son is out of his box and you need to get him back in." And we proceed.

The concept is similar to that which accompanied the drawing in Chapter 1 depicting the child's energy and will to grow as a fast flowing river that needed to be well contained and not dammed:

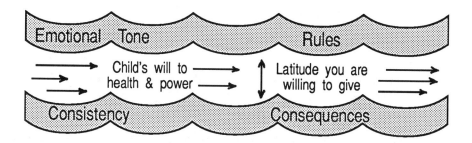

The walls of the "box" are made of the same stuff as the "dike" guiding the flow of the "river" — thick, unbreachable walls that represent your <u>rules</u>, the <u>emotional tone</u> of the way you enforce them, and the <u>consistency</u> with which you enforce the <u>consequences</u>.

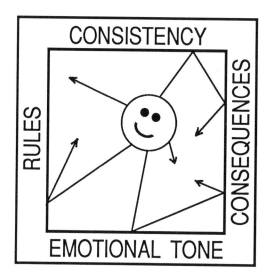

Now your son or daughter is welcome to bounce around in the box anywhere they want to — butt heads with any wall, turn in circles, whatever, but they must stay within those firm boundaries. Most children try to find breaches in the walls and many times are persistent beyond reckoning in trying to get out of the box. When parents allow a child to sneak out, jump out, butt out, cry themselves out, manipulate themselves out or are allowed just to stroll out because the parents don't care or aren't available, there is trouble and confusion for the child. Why? Because kids, unlike my dog, really *want* to be in the "box." The world must seem predictable and secure to a child if she is to make sense out of it and learn what she needs to learn. The craziest children I have encountered are those whose care providers made weak, fuzzy or nonexistent "walls" and then all of a sudden erected hard, harsh ones, later to go back to the weak or absent ones. Those children never feel secure enough to work on the real developmental tasks of childhood because they're too "nervous" about their place in the scheme of the world.

Have you ever said about your child, "He's asking for it!" What is he asking for? Most of the time he's asking for you, as the most important, most powerful person in the world, to structure the world for him, to say to him by your setting firm, reasonable limits and enforcing them that, "Look, son, the world is a fairly predictable, safe place. You go on and do what a kid needs to do to grow up and let us worry about the rest." There is plenty of time for him to realize, as he approaches middle age perhaps, that the world may not be so safe or predictable but by then he'll be able to handle that information.

To accomplish your task, in discipline, of teaching the child to stay "in his box," you have already learned about one of the four components of effective discipline I'm describing, that of *emotional tone* discussed throughout Chapters II and III. *Consistency* is something that requires little explication because your own resolve and level of discomfort with your present situation will probably take care of that. But we do need to talk about *rules* and *consequences* in more detail. We start at the beginning by looking at what defines misbehavior and why kids misbehave.

WHAT IS MISBEHAVIOR?

If you can't tell what misbehavior *is* or *is not*, and your kids are very young, you are going to age rapidly. Perspective is mandatory here since you don't want to take aim at what you perceive as a real problem and it ends up being a decoy.

To begin, I'd like you to take this brief quiz: (all the incidents listed actually took place in our family.)

Please label each statement which you feel is an instance of child misbehavior with an "M":

_____   1. Your baby grabs the spoon out of your hand and tries to feed herself and in the process spills food all over herself.

_____   2. Your three year old "helps" with breakfast and spills juice and cereal all over.

_____   3. The baby knocks the four year old's block tower down and the four year old smacks the baby and makes her cry.

_____ 4. Your two year old empties the ash tray and your husband's/wife's briefcase all over the living room.

_____ 5. Your 18 month old "drops" the spoon off his high chair tray, time after time.

_____ 6. Your three year old takes his dad's clothes out of the closet, tries some on and scatters them around the house.

_____ 7. Your daughter stands up in her high chair all the time and there seems to be nothing you can do to get her to sit down.

_____ 8. Your two year old child says "no" to nearly everything you ask her to do.

_____ 9. Your son dismantled an old but working radio (without your permission) and can't get it back together.

_____ 10. While playing with a rubber ball up against the house, your daughter breaks a window.

_____ 11. You are driving to the coast and your 10 and 12 year old constantly are bickering and fighting in the back seat.

_____ 12. Your 11 year old returns home with two Sunday papers. You gave him money for only one.

_____ 13. Your daughter, eight, refuses to wear all but a

select few tops and jeans. They're beginning to look ratty and sometimes are dirty.

____ 14. Your seven year old can't keep his hands off his four year old brother. Anything is an excuse for a poke or a punch.

____ 15. Your daughter frequently forgets to take out the garbage (her chore).

____ 16. School picture time: your nine year old insists (loudly) that her hair looks wonderful. You know it looks awful. You ask her to change it. She won't.

____ 17. Your son goes out without his jacket after you've asked, then demanded that he put it on.

Time now to check your quiz. If you began to wonder what the extenuating circumstances around the incident were or if you said, "Well, if it happened once as opposed to four or five times, that's different" then you're already developing a useful attitude towards child behavior. Try to remember what has been offered so far in this book about looking at underlying reasons for a given behavior as we discuss these:

1. No "M" here, is there? Why? Is the baby being mean and willful? Of course not. She's just practicing the sort of physical and self-assertion skills that will make her a successful human being.

2. No again. What is the child after? To be "big," to be capable and powerful like adults he sees doing these

same important tasks. To treat the spills as misbehavior would be worse than stupid. Find a way for him to "help" that maintains a clean floor.

3. Now I'll let you get away with either an "M" or nothing because this incident begins to get into an area known as others' safety and rights. First ask yourself what does the four year old want? What more long-term goal is being sought by smacking a defenseless infant? While you must stop this kind of behavior, you must still realize that the four year old is defending her identity, expressing anger at her space being invaded. Knowing this, a wise parent would try to structure the playroom in such a way that the four year old's creations could stand and be displayed for a while.

4. No "M" here unless it happens more than once. The first time means that this young person is trying out big people's tools, practicing. The second time, something else is going on — he's out to get you involved in some sort of struggle, you may bet on it. Then it gets an "M".

5. "Time after time" almost gives this one an "M" but not quite. After the period of intellectual development is past when an object ceases to exist if out of sight, a child becomes fascinated by the sort of cause-effect games that the spoon-drop indicates. Better to remove the spoon and put the child in a better place to practice.

6. Same answer as number 4. If it happens more than once (assuming you gave the proper instructions), it is misbehavior. The first time indicates the same thing being worked on in 4.

7.   Were you tempted by an "M" here? It's close but it doesn't qualify. What is being worked on here? A crucial skill: How does my body work? What can I do with it?   Keeping my daughter in her chair was only possible after I figured out a little reward-type game to keep her there. (By the way, Karin is an outstanding cross country runner in college and she hardly ever stops moving!)

8. No "M" here. Saying "No!" happens about the time a child begins to realize she is not part of her mother and is mobile and verbal enough to express it. It indicates a healthy need to be independent and capable.   "I want to do it myself!" often goes along with the "no." If parents mishandle this stage either by spoiling or by squashing this instinct, what often results is a negativistic and power-obsessed child. A deaf ear to the "no!" and a humane behavior management plan can avoid that.

9. You can't give this one a "M" either, although if you had previously told your son off limits on the radio, then you would. The curiosity expressed here could be best assuaged (after you calm down!) by old equipment that *can* be dismantled and examined. You wouldn't want to dampen the enthusiasm to learn if you have a budding Edison on your hands.

10. Again, no "M" for the first time and an "M" for repeated offenses. There is a lesson to be learned here about what the costs are to damaged property and perhaps having her pay part of the cost would help her realize that lesson sooner.

11. Did you find this hard? I still do. I gave it an "M" because I told my children the car-riding rules and they

still went at it. I stopped the car and refused to go any farther until the bickering stopped. Once I even turned around and went back home. That worked very well. In regards to taking children in the car, ask yourself what gas-saving citizens were asked during World War II: "Is this trip necessary?" A lot of misbehavior results simply from children *not wanting to go*. If that's the case and if your budget or logistics allow it, leave them at home. If they really want to go, then you'll have some leverage and many fewer hassles.

12. Oh, finally an "M" for sure! I said, "Son, you have two papers — I gave you only one dollar. That's called stealing. Take it back now." Everybody I know tried petty theft at one time or another and most report that what really entered their brain pan most effectively was getting caught, and suffering the consequences of it as embarrassing as it is for both child and parents. The best thing most retail stores do for kids is to be very strict about theft.

13. There is no "M" here but if you have an eye over your shoulder on what the neighbors think, your grubby second or third grader will give you fits. After nagging and threatening most of September and October the light bulb went on for me: "This is none of my business! I have many more things to do than worry about Shannon's clothes." Her peers took over. When she got enough negative comments about her appearance, she changed clothes more often.

14. I would put an "M" here because you have already told your seven year old what the rules say about violence and hurting others and he is deliberately flouting them. You still need to find out what the source of his anger is

(besides the mere existence of the four year old) and make sure that the consequences of breaking the rule are logically related and applied soon after he breaks it.

15. Probably an "M" because "forgetting" is hard to accept as an excuse for very long. If her ignoring of her chores has gone on for a while, what you have been doing obviously isn't working. Think about what happens *after* the chore is to be done; it will give you a clue as to what she will miss if the chore is not done first.

16. No "M" for wanting to look awful because it is not interfering with your life and it is, just as the clothes issue, none of your business. Now if you are going to a photographer for a family portrait and shelling out a fair amount for it, I think you have the right to ask that everybody look their best. (Tip off the photographer to suggest that her hair would look a little nicer if she would . . .). But you're better off out of the decision on the school pictures if it threatens to become a power struggle. There are more important issues to go to the mat over.

17. If you have gone ahead and initiated this power struggle, then you may as well win it. This gets an "M" because the child is flouting your requests but a wise parent would take a look first at the weather and, if it were not below freezing or dangerous for him say "Boy, when I go out I'm going to take my coat! It's cold!" And then let the child decide. I am told by physicians that cold air does not cause colds — viruses do. Getting cold and then deciding "I'd better take a jacket next time" works more effectively in the long run to teach responsible decision-making. You won't let your child make a dangerous decision of course, because he is too young to know what

may happen, i.e., even if he felt he could do without a coat today on the Cub Scout picnic and you know that hypothermia is a real possibility, you would make sure the coat goes along in a pack, if nothing else. But average, nonlethal discomfort-producing decisions can and should be left to your child.

My guess is that you did pretty well on this quiz. You knew, I'm sure, before reading this or any other parenting book, that kids don't usually misbehave for the malicious joy it gives them to see you get angry nor do they act up because they're masochists and need to be spanked and yelled at. They misbehave because *they are doing the best they can with the tools they have.*

I said that before but now we're homing in on just what constitutes misbehavior and there are many more gray areas than there are black and white. Children are working at mastering specific developmental tasks at each stage of their lives: babies grab your earring and nose as they find out gradually that they are separate people, first step on the road to becoming independent; cry, smile and babble to practice expressing themselves in various ways so that someday they can communicate effectively; toddlers empty briefcases, jump on sofas and are constantly active while they are developing muscle control in order to eventually master the use of their body for all the marvelous things we do with it, ask endless questions to learn about the world so they can operate in it by themselves; preschoolers hit, threaten, call names, take toys and exclude others because it helps them to learn to play with others and yet get their own way so that someday they can manage the tricky business of being assertive without being a doormat. They make forts out of all the couch pillows to help them understand symbols that stand for real things and be able to manipulate symbols as an adult.

There is a lot going on all the time, isn't there! I rather wish we could be more detailed about the word "misbehavior" — it means "misguided," it means "mistaken," it means "missing the mark," it sometimes (not very often though) means "misanthropic;" it does not mean that the child hates you, does it on purpose every time, or can't "help" it. It just isn't that cut and dried an issue. The more thoroughly you understand the real nature of misbehavior, the better perspective you will have to apply what we have discussed in this book: giving children the right tools through your modeling, communication skills and guidance. If there is a better way for your child to accomplish a growing up task, it's your job to teach it to her. If there isn't a better way, you will have to try to live with the behavior. Usually they will outgrow it.

RULES

Here's a helpful suggestion: sit down with someone else — a friend, spouse, child's teacher or scout leader — and review your rules or the lack of rules. Talk over the need for the rules, their appropriateness, the fairness and their consonance with the age of your kids and your own needs and life-style. Then as you become aware of the holes in your plan and what you want, rewrite the rules with the following guidelines in mind.

Guidelines for Rule Setting

1. Can you tell if the rule has been broken? If you aren't there or if the rule is so vague that you have trouble telling whether your children are following it, you need to change it or get rid of it. Example: "Take out the garbage."

What baskets? When? How often? Which days or weeks? Where to?

2. <u>What are the most closely connected (in time and logic) consequences for breaking the rule?</u> There will be more about consequences in this chapter but, briefly, look for those things of interest and value to the child which would make sense as things to withhold or limit as the most effective consequences. <u>Example</u>: Grounding is probably the best consequence for coming home late because it is logically related and "hurts."

3. <u>Is this a rule that makes sense given the child's age, ability and the resources she has to work with?</u> Make sure, by walking through it with the child if necessary, that she can do it physically and mentally. <u>Example</u>: Don't expect a G.I. barracks type bed-making job from even a ten year old. You will have to accept less than <u>your</u> standards. You will look for consistent, sincere effort.

4. <u>Is the rule detailed enough so the child knows exactly what, how and when the job is to be done or where his body is supposed to be?</u> This is a biggie: describe step by step what "cleaning the garage" entails and don't assume anything; tell what things go where or what "in the house by six o'clock" means to you; make sure that you define the "when" by a watch or a clock. Then there's no room for argument. Examples for number four will follow.

EXAMPLES OF RULES

<u>Fighting with your brother(s)/sister(s).</u> If you are arguing with, yelling at or hitting each other and it goes on longer than a few seconds, I will give you a choice: either stop

the fighting or go to your rooms. You may come out any time after ten minutes when you think you can control yourself. If you fight again, the time will be increased to one hour.

Bedtime. We expect you to be in bed by eight-thirty each school night. That means you are in the bed with your pajamas on and you may have your light on. Your light can stay on until nine o'clock and then must be turned out. If you are not in bed by eight-thirty, you will miss your story and you will go to bed thirty minutes earlier the next night.

Curfew. You are supposed to be in the house and washed for supper by five-thirty. If you aren't you will not watch television that evening. If you are late the next day, you will not be allowed to play with your friends after school for two days.

Doing the dishes. All dishes are to be washed, those from the table, those on the stove and on counters. Dishes should be thoroughly cleaned with the sponge in the soapy water and then rinsed under warm running water. All dishes go in the dish rack to dry. Mom and dad will put them away. (Big children can do this also.) The sinks and counters should be clean of food and the extra food trapped in the baskets should go in the wet-trash basket. Leave the sponge on the back of the sink.

I hope these examples are sufficient for you to get the idea of how clear, detailed and reasonable your rules need to be. Now, to put the cap on this, please remember that no rule is chiseled in stone and unalterable — things change, you change, kids change. So the rules will have to change, too, sometimes. Be on the lookout for signs that the rules need modification, such as extraordinary complaining, foot-dragging or shirking; they may mean you need to re-evaluate the rule.

ENFORCING THE RULES

The skills you have in staying cool and in communication now will be needed in order for you to get the most teaching mileage out of each episode where you must step in and enforce the rules you have made. Here, in brief, is what we have covered so far: 1) lower the emotional tone of each interaction; 2) stay in the adult ego state; 3) resist and replace negative thinking; 4) listen well; 5) realize there are good reasons for the child's behavior; 6) cut your verbal production in half; 7) use the least intrusive words or actions feasible; 8) decide whose problem it is; 9) listen for and accept the child's feelings; 10) talk in a way that indicates that you empathize and are aware of whose problem it is; and 11) send messages of empowerment.

Whew! A lot to remember there but don't panic. Parents tell me that when one of these concepts starts to click, others become easier since they are all very closely connected in philosophy and intent. Here is how one parent enforces rules using many of the skills you have been reading about and practicing.

(The child has just arrived home from school, looking as if he is in a foul mood. He slams the door.)
Mom: "Hi, sport! Nice to see you!"

Son: (Looks, throws coat into the corner of the hall.)

Mom: "Coats go on the hook."

Son: (Screaming) "Why can't you just lay off me! Everybody's screaming at me to do something all day! I hate this!"

Mom: "It sounds like a bad day at school today. Hang your coat up and we can talk if you want."

Son: "This is really stupid — I mean every time I turn around somebody's yelling at me and I didn't do anything."

Mom: "Hmm."

Son: "Teachers are even the stupidest of all adults!"

Mom: "I don't know."

Son: "I'm going downstairs to play with my Nintendo."

Mom: "You're sure welcome to do that as soon as your chores are done. I might even have time to play a little myself before supper."

Son: "Aw, Mom, come on. I've had it!"

Mom: "I believe you. And the chores still need to be done so we can all eat on time. I'll play a game with you about 4:30, OK."

Son: (Walks off.)

Let's analyze the exchange a little. The parent who told me about this very provocative attempt to shove his frustrated feelings off onto his mother was justifiably proud and pleased at how well she did. Something she did extremely well was to sidestep her sons "hooks" like a master bullfighter by refusing to argue, attack or become emotionally threatened by his bad humor. She stood her ground and stated the rules (hanging up coats, doing chores before anything else). She allowed him room to decide — if he wants to talk further about his bad day, if he wants to do his chores or suffer the consequences if he doesn't. She also said something that I never fail to teach parents on their first session with me that I call the "Rule Enforcer Sentence". I'm told it works very well; I know it works well in school settings, too. Here it is:

"You are welcome to _____as soon as_____."

Why does this work so well even when the one you're saying it to is ready to fight? I think because it actually *invites* the person to do something and it is nearly impossible to argue with it. You are prioritizing for this angry person since he can't do a good job of it at the time. This sentence is something you can repeat over and over without feeling like a nag, also. Try saying, "You absolutely cannot have a glass of milk until you have hung up that coat!" about ten times and assess where your head would be after number ten. But I think you could say, "You're welcome to a glass of milk as soon as your coat is on the hook" several times without the same level of anger and self-loathing.

Here's a version of the same sentence you may also find useful when you must say no: Say "yes"!

Child: "Can I have a cookie?"

Parent: "Yes. As soon as supper is finished."

Child: "Can I go out and play?"

Parent: "Yes. As soon as you've cleaned up."

Child: "Dad, can I use the car?"

Parent: "Yes. As soon as you have paid your part of the gas bill."

I first used this sentence several years ago when my youngest, Shannon-of-the- sweet-tooth, asked for the cookie. She looked blankly at me and said, "But... I want it now!" I said, "You can have it after supper," and went about my business.

We'll take this enforcing of rules another step now as we see what goes on when your child insists on pushing the outer limits of his creativity and your patience and *refuses* to follow the rule: (In the previous example where the child did not do the chores but instead went to the playroom and started playing the video game, Mom comes down to speak to him.)

Mom: "Chad, I see you've made a decision."

Son: "What's that?"

Mom: "To ignore the rule that says chores are done before games are played."

Son: "Come on! I just want to take it easy for a while."

Mom: "I understand. And the rule still stands. You have

another choice to make now and here it is: Do the chores or miss video games for ten days. I'll give you five minutes to decide what you will do." (She leaves.)

Mom won't be moved on this, will she? You noticed she still remained an adult and in control and she also did a subtle thing in both these exchanges that you may not have noticed. She replaced the word "but" with the word "and."

> Exchange #1: "I believe you. And the chores still..."
> Exchange #2: "I understand. And the rule still
> stands."

"And" is a more positive word than "but" and it conveys the idea of something further or more to come — like the child doing what he is supposed to do!

"But" reasserts the reality of your own power as a parent, an idea you really don't need to be beating an upset child over the head with. If you find yourself thinking my suggestion of using "and" instead of "but" is hair-splitting, you could be right. Try it for a while before you decide, OK?

A SPECIAL WORD ABOUT MORNING ROUTINE

Before we leave the subject of enforcing rules, I wanted to call your attention to one of the most prolific areas for resistance and power-struggles — all of the decisions and activities around getting up and off to work and school. I say prolific because there are so many things going on in such a short period of time that provide a child with chances to push your buttons or assert her own power. Any child realizes that the clock limits your patience and demands that people *move* in some sort of reasonable, efficient order and if one, small person decides to, she can put a wrench in those works with a minimum of effort. That's why kids so often choose the A.M. routine as their battleground or as their marquee to advertise their needs.

One of my first questions of parents is about the morning routine. About 75% of the time, a large, knowing smile appears on their faces, they nod their heads and say, "Oh, <u>that</u>!" I explain that tomorrow they have a wonderful opportunity to begin re-educating their child about how the real world actually operates and to begin practicing rule enforcement in, at times, a dramatic way. For example, I didn't tell you how Billy's father got out of being Billy's slave, as mentioned in Chapter I. Here's what we planned and Billy's parents did: (I've never heard of this failing, by the way.)

Dad goes upstairs and says, "Billy, time to get up."

No response.

"Billy, I'll see you downstairs for breakfast if you want it."

No response.

Dad goes down to the kitchen, eats his own breakfast and returns. "Well, I see you've decided to sleep in," whereupon he starts putting clothes and shoes into a large paper sack (noisily).

Billy cocks one eye open and says, "What are you doing?"

Dad says, "Oh I figured you didn't want to get dressed here so I'm sending your clothes with you so you can get dressed at school."

Well, as I was told by Dad later, Billy sat upright in the bed and yelled, "You can't do that! They won't let me!"

"Oh, yes," says Dad, "I checked yesterday. You teacher said it was quite alright."

Billy jumps out of bed, grabs the bag from dad and says, "I'll get dressed. Just give me the bag."

"OK," says dad, "breakfast is on in two minutes."

That was the last time Billy refused to get up. Dad said that in the following month he had to rattle the bag a couple of times, but Billy never again demanded the sort of inappropriate service he had been receiving. He tried, though, to transfer the struggle onto the food issue, but again, mom and dad just put the food there and invited him to eat, nothing more. Billy found no one to fight with so he stopped trying. I do know children more persistent who actually do decide to go to school in their pajamas but I've never heard of any who did it more than once.

If a parent decides to try something dramatic I ask them first to have an "empowering chat" with the child the night before and explain the new procedures to them in a context much like this:

"Jennifer, your dad and I have been underestimating you, I think. We've been doing things for you and worrying about stuff that's really none of our business and we think you're old enough and smart enough to take care of those things by yourself. For example, getting up on time and off to school. We're going to leave that to you. Here's what's going to happen tomorrow..."

When you enforce rules in this way you have truly become an ally to your child in her quest to grow up "right" instead of an impediment. You have taught real-world lessons and you have given precious messages about the child's own abilities to be competent and self-directing.

However, if you enforce rules without serious thought and planning about the *consequences* of breaking the rules, you have done only half the work. What happens to a child when he breaks rules or makes bad decisions is what will teach the child whether to try it again and how the world works, so it isn't exaggerating to say that designing or arranging these consequences is a critical job for a parent in discipline.

CONSEQUENCES

Three years ago a father in one of my classes raised his hand and said, "This business about 'consequences' is a bit of verbal gymnastics isn't it? Just an '80's way of saying 'punishment' which has been a bad word for a very long time." We spent several hours differentiating those two ideas and I assure you, there is quite a difference between the two, differences you should be familiar with before you use either one.

What are consequences? First of all, there are two kinds — natural and logical (although the lines between get fuzzy often). *Natural consequences* are those that happen naturally as a result of what a child does — he leaves his bike out, it gets stolen or run over; she goes to school late, she misses recess. *Logical consequences* are those that are imposed by you (or someone) that are logically related to what the child did or did not do — she comes home late, she is grounded, he mouths off to you, he ends up in time-out. With *natural consequences*, the idea is that you *let* the child feel the pain of a bad decision without overprotecting or bailing her out; with *logical consequences*, you *make sure* that he sees that his decision was a bad one.

How do consequences differ from punishment? As stated earlier, mostly the difference lies in the *spirit in which the consequences are applied* but there is more to it, as we'll see.

THE DIFFERENCE BETWEEN CONSEQUENCES AND PUNISHMENT

Punishment requires an adult to judge a child's behavior.
Consequences make the child judge his own behavior.

Punishment creates anger at the person punishing.
Consequences remove everyone but himself for the child to be angry at.

Punishment requires an adult to model anger or irrationality.
Consequences requires an adult to model reasonable, calm behavior.

Punishment teaches a child about power and its coercive use.
Consequences allow a child to feel his own power.

Punishment requires the adult to decide.
Consequences requires the child to decide.

Punishment requires the child to "pay for" a mistake. **Consequences** requires the child to figure out what to do the next time.

GROUNDING AS A CONSEQUENCE

Parents who have used these rather simple guidelines say that they work to keep the rules reasonable and the enforcing of them in proper perspective. Please feel free to be creative and sensible about the consequences you impose for misbehavior. I tend to cringe every time a parent says to me, "By golly, I grounded her for two months! She'll learn to do her chores on time!" Trying to tell a parent such as this that he is on another planet in regards to discipline is sensitive business. Grounding applied to all offenses shows a lack of thought; what's worse, it creates so much resentment in the groundee that it creates another more serious problem between parent and child. Try not to fall into that black and gaping hole. Again, consequences must be related in *time* and *logic* to the offense. Grounding is related to rules about coming and going and is an appropriate consequence for breaking those rules — perfect, as a matter of fact. Grounding is not in the least related to fighting , forgetting chores, mouthing off, foot-dragging or insensitivity.

TIME-OUT AS A CONSEQUENCE

Time-out still is one of the best and most often used consequences for misbehavior because it works and is so easy to relate to the offense in time and logic. What we discussed earlier in this book in regards to children's behavior being ultimately tied to their need for social recognition applies to the efficiency of time-out. To be included in the family activity, play activity, classroom activity, church activity or even any two person interaction is a child's lifeline to learning and feeling valuable. When her behavior is inappropriate, selfish, destructive, insensitive, willful, or careless and it affects others by interfering with their (or your) rights in some way, removing her from the company of others makes good sense and teaches her quickly and directly that the behavior will not be tolerated.

How is time-out best handled? The most effective way, one which follows the philosophy put forth here of allowing a child as many choices as possible, is to demand that the child go to time-out and give them a set time to stay, say ten minutes, and tell them that any time after that *when they feel they can act properly*, they may return to the activity. Your contingency for further misbehavior is another, longer time-out, say thirty minutes to an hour. Same rules for leaving time-out as the first time. Time-out is *thinking* and *planning* time for your child and if you enforce time-out in a firm, calm manner, it won't be a time for smoldering resentment and making plans for revenge. Remember, your tone of voice and manner will tell the child whether time-out is retribution by you or the logical end to a dumb decision on her part.

SPANKING AS A CONSEQUENCE

What about spanking? The question is one you must first counter with another question: How long can you continue to spank a child if it is your main method of discipline — till they're ten, twenty? OK, probably not even until ten, correct? So when will you stop using spanking and what will you replace it with?

I seldom spanked, but when I did it was like adding

an exotic spice to a stew — just enough, at just the right time. That's what I will suggest here: if you use spanking, use it sparingly and when you need the emphasis most. If you use it as your main tool, you'll be in for enough trouble to keep you busy into your old age. The best advice is, however, not to use it at all.

CONSEQUENCES YOU SHOULD NEVER USE

By this time, it probably isn't necessary to explain why the following consequences should be avoided. I think you are getting the picture by now.

Don't

- use sarcasm
- belittle
- threaten without following through
- wheedle
- cajole
- apologize for doing what a responsible parent should
- withhold love and affection
- pit one child against the other (more on this later)
- whine
- swear
- anything else that diminishes your dignity or that of your child

CONSISTENCY

In the beginning of this chapter it was stated that consistency will come to you if you are determined enough to really change what you are doing now. You need to know that even if you blow it in disciplining children part of the time, that's much better than being inconsistent. Inconsistency is just a polite way of saying you either don't care or you are not trying, neither of which is very comforting once you know a better way. Being wrong at times is preferable to inconsistency; being unreasonable or petulant 10% of the time is better than being wish-washy. Even if you think you might be making an error in *what* you are doing in discipline situations, bear in mind *how* you go about doing it is probably more important. And consistency is the underpinning of all of the various *hows* that you are practicing.

TOTAL RESISTANCE

What happens when the child refuses to go to time-out or goes there but won't stay? What do you do with the child who is perfectly willing to miss school or be late rather than get up on time? How do you handle a child who says, "I don't care." to any consequence you impose? Our discussion of discipline will need to include some thoughts regarding "when nothing works."

The first concept to remember is that very discouraged children act in unproductive ways most of the time. These children will resist change for the better with all their might because: 1) their self-concept won't allow it; and 2) they don't feel capable of it. Very discouraged children will attempt total resistance far more often than children who are not so discouraged. So before you plan any strategy to overcome total resistance, you must keep in mind that to overcome it in the long run you need to be rigorously using the communication and discipline techniques you've been learning. These will always form the backbone of your discipline plan because they turn around the negative, demeaning messages that a discouraged child has had far too many of already.

The second step is, of course, to have a plan of action ready for total resistance which allows you to enforce the rules and still maintain the dignity of everyone involved. That's hard but it can be done. The fact that you have physical power over the child is obvious to both of you and you will need to use that power in a benevolent way just as you use your emotional power in your interactions. If time-out is the logical, humane consequence for an infraction, then you must see to it that you child *goes* and *stays* there, even if you have to carry her. If she will not stay there, you must again see to it that she doesn't leave. That may mean locking the door. Many parents object to this. I understand why — it's an extreme measure, one which I only used once with my own children. But total resistance is not very common. Most parent-child relationships have grown on a mutual realization of the role and power of each party and have been nurtured by positive communication. Children who totally refuse to do what is reasonable have already progressed past a point of discouragement — "What's the use?" — that will require much effort, perhaps physical restraint being one of the necessary parts of your plan.

If your child is too old and too large to forcibly take to time-out, you're too late. What has caused the rebellion has had too many years to become a pattern and you won't change that with ordinary means discussed here. You very likely need to see a family counselor in order to find the reasons for the total resistance and ways to get all of you back on track. With children who have not had such negative input, firm, nonhurting physical restraint sends a couple of important messages: 1) "I am safe. My parents will take care of me and see that I do the right thing; and 2) the world is predictable. Adults are supposed to be in charge."

Most children do respond to the messages of empowerment that you have learned in this book. And even when they don't and you must physically assert your authority, it can also be done in a loving, nonpunitive manner. But frequent total resistance is a warning signal that you may have some more serious problems with your child that could require professional help.

PUTTING YOUR PLAN INTO ACTION

At this point you are ready to begin addressing some of the most stubborn behavior problems you deal with. Using the "behavior box" chart shown below, pick one issue that seems to have been resistant to change, no matter what you have tried, and do those things listed on the next page.

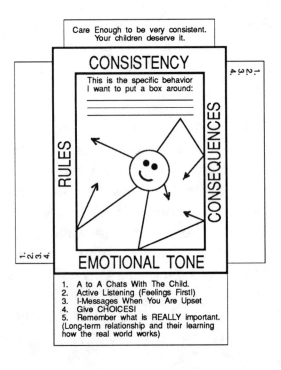

(A full-sized copy of the chart is located in the Appendix.)

1. Sit down with someone you trust, especially another parent who has read this book, and discuss *what* the problem is and *why* you think it has become one.

2. Define exactly what the behavior is that you want to change and write it in the lines provided at the top of the box.

3. Decide what the rules are about the issue you're working on. Write those in the space provided and in your "empowering chat" with the child, spell them out clearly.

4. Do the same for the consequences part and write what the positive and negative consequences will be if the child chooses one course of action or another. Again, clearly communicate that to your child.

5. On the bottom of the chart under "emotional tone", go through the five steps listed there. If you do, it will ensure that the talking and disciplining will be done in the spirit of love, concern and helpfulness that ensures success.

After you see your child's behavior change as a result of your efforts, this process of identification of the problems and a reasoned, well-thought-out plan to attack it will become a pattern for you to use for any succeeding issues, as an artist or engineer would use a template time and again on work of a similar nature. Behavior problems have their roots in such fundamental human needs that their solutions lie in addressing those needs in a consistent, humane way. That's why this plan will work and you don't need to have a "prescription" for every little hassle that arises. It just takes *practice* and *self-discipline*. It is not complicated at all, but it is difficult because of our own histories and deep emotional involvement with our children.

Try this plan today. It will work for you and will give you what perhaps has been very elusive — the ability to handle discipline effectively and also feel sane most of the time.

The final concept necessary here is that of the "size" of these behavior boxes. In each case, there is a decision to make regarding how much room you will allow a child to have over any behavior. For example, at one extreme a box around the behavior "drinking and driving" would look this way:

This is NO room at all. It just isn't going to happen if you can help it. The box looks the same for "playing with fire" or "experimenting with drugs" or "staying out all night." There is no room in the box for these kinds of behavior.

For an issue such as "sibling hassles," there has to be room because you can't stop these. However, your family values and personal tolerance may make the box for this behavior pretty small, such as this compared, say to another family's tolerance where open, loud conflict is much more acceptable due to their cultural and historical experience, where the box would be bigger:

But whether collapsed or very large, the limits are still there and the ways they are enforced are the same.

CHAPTER V: SELF-ESTEEM

Self-esteem is a slippery concept, one that I believe is widely misunderstood among both educators and parents. The word implies the effect of nearly *everything* that happens to a person from the time of conception and that makes this complex topic one which leaves itself open to much confusion. Some define the word as something that can be "given" to a person by parents or by schools or churches or scout troops or soccer teams; others may say it is a set of skills that allows a person to cope with the difficulties of life and struggle against a tough world out there. Recently, the subject of self-esttem has arisen on a national and regional level as we compare our children's academic achievement to that of children in other countries. The thrust of much of the concern with the effects of high and low self-esteem, as I see it, has more to do with the tendency of public policy to attempt short-term, surface solutions to problems that are fundamental, broad-based and long-term. In other words, we cannot fix problems of low achievement and high drop-out rates with a course on self-esteem in high school. The roots of self-esteem run far deeper that that and are embedded in our social structure and how each one of us relates to it. In addition, these roots are obviously connected to our intimate relationships in our families.

Consequently, it is hard to say something coherent and useful to parents about self-esteem, but I feel the need to make this topic somewhat intelligible and useful for you since that is a goal throughout the book.

A WORKING DEFINITION

Before we delve into the roots of self-esteem as it develops in families, here is a definition of it as I have watched my own children and others over the last thirty years.

1. Self-esteem cannot be separated from the social environment a child lives in. If it is unsafe and debilitating and non-nurturing, it doesn't matter what courses or slogans or exhorations a child is subject to — his self-confidence will suffer.

2. Self-esteem is vitally connected to what a child does and how she sees herself interacting with the world — neighborhood, school, community, country. If the feedback she gets is that she is powerful, valuable, needed and capable, she will think highly of herself and her abilities. We must not dupe ourselves into believing that racism or poverty can be overcome by a "feel good" slogan or a self-esteem curriculum in grade school.

3. Self-esteem grows from very early roots in a child's family and those family roots create abilities in children to self-manage, succeed at tasks and cope with life's inevitable setbacks. If a child is loved and nurtured and allowed to experiece success as a result of her own efforts, she will be confident that she can do more as she gets older and will feel proud and capable. If she is talked to and disciplined in humane ways, she will feel worthy of being respected and successful. If she is allowed (by parents and society as a whole) to accomplish socially meaningful tasks, she will find joy and satisfaction in operating fully and independently in the world.

THE FAMILY CONNECTION

Since a detailed account of how families affect self-esteem is beyond the intent of this book, what follows is really a summary of ideas you may find more developed in good books such as Jean Clarke's *Self-Esteem: A Family Affair*; Dorothy Briggs' *Your Child's Self-Esteem*; or Clarke's and Connie Dawson's *Growing Up Again*. I encourage you to consult these books.

We all come from families in which we were teated in a variety of ways: lovingly and caringly; cooly and neutrally; punitively and brutally; rigidly and neglectfully; or some combination of these styles. We had no say in how we were treated because we were helpless babies and rather powerless as growing children. Depending upon how we were loved or not loved, cared for or not cared for, affirmed or not affirmed, we all *absorbed* certain messages about our basic worth that formed the very core of the way we felt about ourselves. These messages are persistent and very hard to change, the reason for the need for parents to be aware of what effects their words and actions have. These are "Life Messages" and they are listed below under the respective parenting regimes that produce them.

Rigid, Brutal or Uncaring	Supportive, Caring & Involved
The child will internalize...	The child will internalize...
"I am not worth much."	"I am valued."
"I should not be here."	"I am welcome here."
"No one cares."	"People care about me."
"I am loved only for what I do."	"I am loved no matter what."
"I'm not loved."	"I am loved."

"I am not capable."	"I can do it."
"I am not strong."	"I am strong."
"I am not good enough."	"I am a good person."
"Life is bad."	"Life is OK."
"It's useless to even try."	"I can do it even if it's hard."

A "Life Message" is not unchangeable but you must understand that the message is part of him, an unconscious part that will affect every decision he makes about himself until he receives new or different information that can alter how he feels. Sometimes that new information "gets in" to his consciousness and sometimes it doesn't — it depends on luck, life experiences and fate, it seems to me. People do change and overcome some awful breaks in their childhood. But those who escape the very negative or destructive life messages imprinted on them in their malleable early years are certainly in the minority. Most people are not forunate enough to be able to avoid literally living out their low opinion of themselves.

The messages you see in both columns are as programmed into people as any given to a computer and are vastly more difficult to re-program. How will you be able to succeed and feel good about yourself if you are convinced, to the bottom of your soul, that you are worthless and bad? As has been stated here before, people become what they are told they are, what they are expected to be. When you look at the life messages in the left column, you may well wonder, "How could *any* parent be so cruel and unfeeling and downright stupid?"

The answer lies in 1) the way the parent was raised herself and 2) the fact that most of the words and actions that produce negative Life Messages are *not done consciously* by a parent. People's upbringing creates their unconsciously-held Life Messages and they pass these on also to their children without knowing it. There are psychological mechanisms at work (wonderfully detailed in the works of Alice Miller) which make awareness of past pain and trauma very difficult to unearth. Pain which is not brought to consciousness and acknowledged and worked through *will be passed on* to someone else and the most readily available, vulnerable people, of course, are one's own children. That is how these messages continue to create problems for many of us.

Last week a parents' class was asked to offer adjectives that describe a person with high self-esteem.

The list is produced below exactly as they gave it to me:

resilient	giving	responsible
open	adventurous	responsive
creative	strong	courageous
happy	positive	committed
flexible	honest	calm
integrated	thoughtful	spontaneous
loving	caring	inventive

Most of us are aware of what qualities must be "built-in" in order for a child to become fully functional, to feel strong enough and happy enough to use all of her God-given abilities. But our own limitations often get in the way of building those qualities into our children.

If you are reading this book, you have already made a decision to change some of your behavior and attitudes, which means that the following suggestion will, I am confident, fall on fertile soil. So here it is: if you want to enhance your child's self-esteem, find out about how you were raised, what Life Messages you received and which ones are causing you and your child the most trouble, and how you can begin to re-program yourself. As you know, there are already volumes written on how to go about this process, some of which are listed in the back of this book. Changing your own patterns is at once the most challenging and the most satisfying project you will ever take on. Old pain does not want to surface. When it does, it makes us so uncomfortable that our first instinct is to stuff it back where it came from. Don't do it! The joy of knowing that you can raise a child free of many of the negative messages you received is worth all the necessary upset that change will bring. When you realize why you act the way you do, you can see clearly what you need to do next when your child touches a piece of the old pain and you are tempted to react in ways that run very deep in you.

About a month ago a parent in a current seminar asked this: "You said that our very committment to changing almost guarantees that our kids will grow up OK, that we could leave now and feel comfortable with how we'll raise our children. Why should we stay, then?"

I answered his excellent question with this story: There is a friend of mine who has about everything a person in his late thirties can want, I suppose: a good relationship , kids he co-parents with his second wife, a career and in general a staisfying life. The sad part, as I see it, is that my friend has his track shoes on and is constantly looking over his shoulder as he runs and runs. It seems that he can never be satisfied with himself or his life. It's not that he is miserable, destructive or suicidal — he simply cannot believe that he can allow himself happiness or satisfaction. Whatever talents and accomplishments he has (and they are considerable), there is always with him the sense of not being quite good enough or deserving enough to just "be" and let that suffice. What I know of this fine man is that his childhood was filled with messages that he was not OK the way he was, that he was not loveable just for himself, that he had always to prove that he was worthy of love and care. He had to earn it, day after day, year after year.

And so my answer to the question of "Why learn more about parenting and child behavior and about yourself?" is that you have a chance to save your child from perhaps 20 or 30 years of pain and self-doubt. You can avoid putting up roadblocks to his happiness you may have had to struggle with. Teaching children about life, about love, about real-world consequences is hard enough and life itself will be painful enough without your putting additional burdens on your kids due to ignorance or lack of awareness.

My friend is lucky that he had enough care and support to allow himself to become functional but not so fortunate in how he was imprinted with a "Somehow Defective" stamp on his soul. He works at it through periodic therapy but it is an uphill battle and I love him for his courage. Purifying and heroic it may well be — but I'd just as soon save my own children from 20 or 30 years of that if I can.

The remainder of this chapter contains descriptions, suggestions and ideas to help you gain perspective on your child's feelings of self-worth and to put into practice concepts that will make a difference in how he views himself. These ideas won't do the job completely, but they are a good place to begin.

CHARACTERISTICS OF LOW SELF-ESTEEM AND HIGH SELF-ESTEEM

What follows are lists of what you can look for in regards to your child's feelings about herself. Please keep in mind that these behaviors, to be accurate indicators, must be observed *consistently over time*. Everyone periodically feels stupid and worthless — try backing out of your driveway and into the side of the neighbor's car if you want an example — but it doesn't last too long or happen very frequently in people with solidly positive feelings about themselves. Remember to look for *patterns* of behavior; those will tell you what you want to know.

A child whose self-esteem is LOW will *consistently...*

1. feel that others don't value him. He finds little satisfaction with friends, often feels rejected and left out by his peers, and will complain that he has no friends or that no one likes him. You will not be able to talk the child out of this belief and if it is a pattern over time, you need to look at why.

2. become easily frustrated and defensive. Even small projects may become major sources of frustration for her if she runs into a difficulty that is not easily overcome. She will avoid looking hard at her own part in the problem and has little persistence to stay at it until it is solved.

3. avoid anxiety-producing situations. The low self-esteem child will not want to face situations that demand of him a show of competence, such as tests at school or contests where he thinks his profound inadequacies will be on public display.

4. be easily influenced by other people. She will find it hard to say no, especially to peers. This, of course, gets

dangerous the older the child becomes. She will do things which she knows are wrong or even bad for her but her own sense of worth and confidence are not strong enough to endure the derision and/or exclusion from the group which may follow a "no."

5. feel powerless. You'll find this child often using the words "never" and "can't." Even the smallest hassles, like a lost book or broken toy, become showcases for his deeply pessimistic view of himself and his belief in his own inability to affect or change things very much.

6. put down himself and his abilities. This child will not accept the worth of much that he does and will often say so. "Nothing I sew ever looks any good." Again, you won't be able to talk him out of this and it is a consistent pattern you will look for.

7. show a narrow band of feelings. A person must risk in order to show his emotions to any degree and very low self-esteem children don't want to do that. It's too scary. These are the children of whom parents and teachers often say, "It doesn't matter what we do to punish him — he doesn't care. Nothing seems to get through to him."

8. refuse to accept blame or responsibility. She will seldom, if ever, admit to shortcomings or failures or even small mistakes. "I couldn't do the dishes because you never showed me where the new glasses go." Of course, this is hard even for those people who have strong self-esteem most of the time. A child who feels she is of little value can't risk the admission of imperfection — there just isn't enough room in her ego for that.

A child whose self-esteem is HIGH will consistently...

1. <u>act independently.</u> The child will initiate things without a lot of prodding or coaxing. New tasks are usually a challenge that she takes on with very little whining or fearfulness. Her confidence in herself will often get her into situations you may not even like, but there's nothing malicious in it — she is just trying out her abilities.

2. <u>feel as if she can affect other people.</u> She will want to "teach" other children how to do things and has little fear of entering social situations that are new. She is able to relate to these new people without being overly bossy or passive and can usually handle cooperative activities well (after the age of six or so).

3. <u>tolerate frustration.</u> Although you may hear him gripe a good deal about difficult or complicated tasks, this child will normally stick with it and try to figure it out. One mistake or failure won't often send him away in tears, giving up.

4. <u>show a fairly large range of feelings.</u> She will feel comfortable about letting the world see both the unpleasant and "nice" side of her personality. You will generally know where this child is, emotionally, although you must remember that children are sometimes simply "born that way." Each is different. However, you won't find a high self-esteem child consistently in the gray or seemingly neutral emotional zone.

5. <u>assume responsibility.</u> Remembering that nearly all children will try hard to keep out of trouble or blame, this child will accept responsibility of both negative and positive

nature — the blame for mistakes or the jobs that must be done to make the household run well. He is strong enough to feel that he is capable of accepting those responsibilities.

6. <u>take pride in herself and her accomplishment.</u> You won't hear a lot of self-criticism from a child with high self esteem because she believes in herself. The pictures, drawings, chores accomplished or favors done for people are all projections of herself and her comments about them are comments about her as she sees herself.

I feel the need to repeat what was said earlier about self-esteem: it waxes and wanes, it is low in some areas and high in others (just as yours and mine is), and *all* children will show *all* of the above characteristics at one time or another. Rather than focusing on or worrying about your child exhibiting one or more of the low self-esteem indicators (please don't!), assess the long-term pattern of the child's actions.

The facts seem to be, from the research done on self-esteem, that it is very stable over time; that is , it doesn't change a whole lot. If you consider why for a few minutes, it makes sense — my own image of myself is all I have. If I give that up, what am I left with? I'll hang on tightly to a bad self-image because that is better and safer to me than none at all. In the past twenty years, I've seen many examples of that stability, the most vivid example being a boy I'll call Donald.

Donald was in trouble nearly every day in his second grade classroom. He was defiant, verbally obscene and often physically abusive to other children. There was very little that worked with him because his early deficits were so great that the school setting couldn't adequately remedy them. But we tried and he taught me a lesson about the tenacity of a person's view of himself.

At that time I had read the advice given by psychologists that cautioned against praising very discouraged children because, they said, it would often backfire. I either forgot or ignored the advice when one morning, the day after one of Donald's few good days, I saw him in the hall and said, "Donald, your teacher told me that you behaved well all day yesterday. Way to go. I'm impressed!"

Donald looked at me and said nothing. At 9:15, soon after class began, I got a frantic call from the teacher.

"Jon, you have to come down here and get Donald. He's lost it!"

I went to his room and Donald was snarling in the corner on the rug, swearing. He had taken a sharp pencil and stabbed his deskmate in the face with it for no reason anyone could see. One of the reasons for his outburst (I found out later after trying the praise routine twice more and experiencing similar aftermaths) was that I told him something — "You're a good boy" — that ran so counter to his own belief — "I'm a bad boy" — that he set out to reduce the conflict between those two views and prove me wrong. He was determined to hang on to his image of himself, to the point of harming others.

We did make some progress with Donald but only after we learned not to praise him directly but to reward him quietly and indirectly. Even though he was an extreme example of this stability of self-view (Donald needed serious psychiatric care and later received it), I want you to understand the really good news about it: the quality of relationships in a child's life and his experiences can greatly influence and change his self-esteem. You have been reading and practicing how to do that in the first four chapters of the book.

If you'd like to change your title of "parent" to a more upscale one, you could call yourself a "Child's Life-Success Facilitator." Imagine a business card with that printed on it!

25 THINGS TO DO EVERY DAY ABOUT YOUR CHILD'S SELF-ESTEEM

It might be helpful for you to copy these suggestions and post them somewhere visible to refer to on a daily basis, especially if you have not been in the habit of affirming and stroking your child regularly. These may help you establish some effective behavior changes in a shorter time.

1. Listen to your child and accept his feelings even if you don't particularly like the ones expressed.

2. Accept the child as a separate, unique and special person with a life that is, and will be increasingly separate from your own.

3. Be a positive model for him. Treat yourself well and take care of yourself in a healthy way. He is likely to become much like you.

4. Give her respsonsibilities and independence of action appropriate to her age. Create space for her to exercise new-found skills and ideas.

5. Establish firm limits, rules and controls so that he can begin to establish his own by the time he is ready and the world demands it of him.

6. When you either praise or criticize, be <u>specific</u> about it. Global statements that are perceived as "good boy" or "bad boy" are confusing and counterproductive.

7. Always make it known that,"I like you but sometimes I don't like what you do" when things go wrong.

8. Tell your child the truth. It is very hard to lie to a child for long and be successful. It's demeaning to be deceived.

9. Respect her feelings, needs and desires when decisions are being made that affect her.

10. Let go of your unrealistic ambitions or fantasies about what he should be now or will become. He is wonderful right now, just as he is.

11. Own your own feelings and problems by using "I-messages" instead of "you-messages."

12. Remember that advice is cheap and usually not wanted; be careful about overdirecting when just being there and listening or answering questions will do just as well.

13. Say, "I love you." a lot.

14. Hug a lot.

15. Smile a lot.

16. Teach her to anticipate the consequences of her actions; i.e., "What will happen if you do that?" "What can you think of that might help?"

17. *Don't compare your child to any other child, even siblings.*

18. *Provide choices from as early an age as you can, starting with things as simple as what to wear and going up to what college to attend.*

19. *Don't ridicule or shame a child, in public or in private.*

20. *Surprise a child with a special treat or activity when they least expect it.*

21. *Teach social graces and good manners to show children how to positively affect others.*

22. *Share yourself with your child — your interests, plans, hopes; it's hard not to like someone you know so well.*

23. *Involve your child in a variety of activities — physical, intellectual and creative. Let them find avenues for success and satisfaction.*

24. *Don't overinvolve yourself in her business; don't overprotect her from the legitimate hurts and bruises that life will deal her.*

25. *Teach him how to solve problems by breaking them into smaller parts so they can be managed.*

FAMILY MEETINGS: THE BEST WAY TO STRUCTURE POSITIVE CHANGE

If you aren't meeting together as a family on regular basis right now, resolve to start as soon as you can. Family meetings are the best way I know to begin to put into action many of the ideas you find in this book. Family meetings, conducted under strict rules for communicatiion and participation, will do several things for you.

1. It helps you bond as a group and feel your closeness and interdependence.

2. It teaches the skills of participation in a group.

3. It teaches people how to communicate about important matters in a structured, positive way.

4. It makes real the idea that each person's presence and input is valuable.

5. It gives form and direction to your effort to raise self-esteem by including children as important and valuable contributors to the family unit.

6. It teaches skills and attitudes that are valuable life-skills when children leave the family.

Dolores Curran (*Traits of a Healthy Family*, 1983) describes traits of healthy families as reported to her by mental health professionals, social workers and educators. From her list, (which was in priority order) here are the first five.

1. Communicates and listens.

2. Affirms and supports one another.

3. Teaches respect for others.

4. Develops a sense of trust.

5. Has a sense of fair play.

These traits will not automatically develop themselves. You need some structured way to make sure that each family member receives the positive messages implicit in these traits and the family meeting is the best way I know to lay the groundwork for that to happen. Sharing, planning and problem-solving require a high degree of skill in *talking and listening,* in *respecting* each others' opinions, in *trusting* each one's abilities and intentions. It becomes clear to all, over time, what family values are and how important every person is to the unique make-up of that unit. When everybody is pulling on the same ropes, it is hard for any one person to feel alone or outcast.

In recent research regarding children who choose drug use and those who refuse to take that way out, it was very clear that the primary reason for a child's saying "No" to drugs was that "it would hurt my family." The same family bonding is responsible for a teen's ability to resist peer pressure in other areas. My experience with family meetings is that they provide a template for this bonding process that can be applied to situations outside of the family meeting. It's pretty difficult to meet and talk respectfully and share feelings and plans on Sunday and then forget how to do those things on Wednesday. It's an axiom in counseling that growth is one-way: once you experience the satisfaction that healthy change brings, you just don't go back to more painful, inefficient ways of relating to each other.

Below is an outline of how to run family meetings.

I. <u>Basic Ground Rules</u>

A. Everyone in the household group, related or not, participates.

B. Meetings are regularly scheduled. Each person needs to know just how long they must wait to air their problem. The time must be agreeable to all. Weekly meetings are suggested.

C. Rules must be agreed upon and followed. One rule should provide for a chairman and secretary and these jobs are rotated, even to the children.

D. An open forum is mandatory. Any person is free to speak about anything that is on his/her mind — complaints, ideas, opinions.

E. A guarantee of no interruptions is mandatory when any one person has the floor. This is sometimes very hard to do but it must be guaranteed for all.

F. Absolute freedom of expression is guaranteed. No topic, no feelings are taboo. No one is chastised or put down for what they say however unpleasant it may seem.

G. There will be no fear of consequences after the meeting. The family council is a "safety zone."

H. All members, regardless of age, are treated equally.

I. There is no voting: to reach a decision all members must agree.

II. <u>Watch Out For</u>

A. One person who wants to dominate the meeting. Every other member must listen to the speaker so the chairman will recognize each one in turn.

B. In a crisis, you all probably can't make a good decision anyway. Cool off. Wait for the family meeting.

C. Family council is not just a gripe session. It is a place for an individual to bring his problems for the entire group to deliberate on what they can do to help solve them. Planning fun activities should also be part of family meetings.

D. Often, children may make decisions which appear to be in error, due to their inexperience. This is no time for "I told you so" from adults — more effective is to allow the children to find out for themselves.

E. Once a decision is made, it must stand until the next meeting. If one person does not live up to the agreement, others have the right not to also; i.e., if clothes aren't put in the right place, mom (or whomever) has the right not to wash them.

F. No one person is responsible for the smooth working of the family — not mom, not dad, not any one child. All share responsibility.

G. There is no living together without problems and conflict. These need to be addressed and solved and worked on. Giving up will not accomplish this.

Getting teenagers to buy into the idea of a family

meeting may be difficult. If they resist it, there are a couple of ways to encourage their participation: one is to simply say, "Bill, this is real important to me. I need your help on this and I promise it won't be long or stupid, OK? I really want you there." Another way would be to bargain: "Look, Jamie, it's really important to me that we meet together . It will help our family. I'll tell you what, you do me a favor and I'll do you one." When teens see that they will be listened to and not lectured or asked their opinion instead of being dictated to, they will participate, even though you may have to overlook some skepticism or obnoxiousness at first. Younger children don't usually need to be coaxed to participate. Just gear part of the meeting to their ability to contribute.

The best suggestion I have run across to begin the meetings is to designate a certain amount of money for a family outing and then make the focus of the first meeting how it should be spent. Later meetings can take up the usual topics of chore schedules, etc., but the first one will set the tone positively if it is lighter and more fun.

SELF-ESTEEM AND THE USE OF PRAISE

Children's behavior needs praise if they are to learn about their abilities and feel needed and competent. However, many adults don't separate the *behavior* of a child from the *child himself*, in the praising or the correcting of behavior. That failure to separate the action from the actor can cause some unpleasant side-effects. Praise which broadly comments on a child's worth as a person can be destructive, even when you don't mean it to be, i.e., "Good Boy!" In addition, if we are trying to encourage our children to be self-starting and self-evaluating, how can that happen if <u>we</u> are the primary source of evaluating their behavior and accomplishments? We will need to teach them to praise and encourage themselves, also, especially as they get older and the world tends to give them fewer and fewer strokes.

Some years ago I worked in a school where the principal operated on the theory that everyone would do their best if he praised them often and effusively. Not a bad idea on the surface of it, but it didn't work. I would hear praise from him about things I had done that I considered either ordinary or less than my best stuff. It was confusing and also, I found, somewhat irritating. I was able to judge at that point in my career how effective I was most of the time and the real message I received from the praise which was overdone and/or inaccurate was not very positive — it felt as if he really didn't know or care to find out the details of my job or if there were any strengths or weaknesses he noted that should be built upon or changed. Overall, his message, as well-meaning as it was, came across negatively to me. It was one of benign neglect, of only passing interest in me and my work. What I wanted I received later in my career from a woman who gave me very specific feedback about my job skills, both the positive and the negative. And strangely enough, even though she was not the open "cuddly" sort of person that my effusively-praising principal was, I liked and respected her enormously. Why? Because I had solid evidence of her sincere interest in my growth and well-being. That's hard to ignore.

Let's talk about how children may view praise. Last week I was observing some of my counselees (fifth graders) working in a peer-tutoring situation with a kindergarten class and as I wandered about the room, a girl at the easel stopped me and said, "Look what I painted!" It was difficult to stifle my urge to say, "My that's good!" Instead

I said, "You have a brilliant blue house, with smoke coming out, a yellow sun and a girl with yellow hair. I like the red ribbon in her hair!"

She smiled and said, "No, that's not a ribbon; it's a bird. It's a nice picture." She continued painting the blue sky, still smiling.

Why didn't I say, "You're a good painter." or "What a good picture!"? For several reasons:

1. What is she thinking? "Oh, this isn't really good. What's he talking about? Is he a liar?" or "Well, I'm a good painter, but he probably doesn't know about my bad temper." I would rather not be in the position of judge. I'd rather she did it.

2. What is the point of my praise? To make her feel good? To establish myself in a one-up position? I would rather she learn to praise herself because she'll be needing to do that all too soon.

3. What do I know? Am I an art critic, or a sweep-the-floor critic, or an eating habits critic? Hardly, I'm a teacher and a friend and I'd like it very much if this enthusiastic, intelligent child grew up to be able to look clearly at her own abilities without depending on people like me for her opinions. If she would like to become a serious artist, there will be plenty of chances for serious artistic criticism, but if I stifle her own ability to paint or turn her efforts into a game between a "praiser" and "praisee," she might never feel competent enough to get to that highly developed place in her career.

So, what I will do with praise is to describe what I see, what I appreciate, what I am aware of and then let the child's own intelligence and capacity for self-evaluation do the rest. You already know how this works because you are learning to use "I-messages;" it's basically the same idea:

Son: "How'd you like the game, Dad?"

Dad: "I just saw you hit two doubles, catch a really hard liner and a lot of outs. Wow!"

Son: "Hey, was I great or was I great?"

Dad: "I'll bet you're really proud of yourself!"

Son: "Man, did you see me whack that last one?"

Dad: "I did. You know what impressed me? You looked like you were trying hard on every play. I appreciate that."

Consider what the child may think the next time if you said a lot of "good boy" sorts of praise and the next game was full of mistakes: "If I was a good boy last week when I played well, what am I this week when I played badly? A bad boy?"

I'm suggesting, given what I've observed about the way kids understand things, that you consider the preceding question carefully. If you are always using that sort of judgmental, nonspecific praise when things go well, what will the child believe when things don't go well, as they always do? And when you are specific about aspects of a child's performance or production, you are teaching him how to analyze what needs work without your becoming the judge. Many adults' careers depend on their ability to do that kind of analysis and problem solving about his and/or others' performance. It seems to me that if you are truly interested in giving your child a leg up in the world, helping her to become self-evaluating and thus, self-praising, is a fine way to do it.

GETTING AHEAD?   EXPECTATIONS FOR YOUR CHILD

David Elkind (*The Hurried Child*, 1988) has described very well, and to me somewhat chillingly, how our society has put so much pressure on its children to perform, to grow up too fast and to omit parts of their own necessary development as children in a misguided, destructive quest for status (theirs and ours), "keeping up" with whomever is breathing down our necks or a neurotic worry that there is something our there the child will miss or fall behind in if we don't push, push, push. I would like to put into perspective that normal desire of parents to want their children to achieve and be happy because your expectations have such a strong bearing on the child's self-esteem.

What has been put forth in this book about how to raise a responsible, healthy child — being nurturing, firm and expecting high standards of behavior — does in no way mean that parents expect *more than is possible, reasonable and good for the child*. That is a tall order for most parents. Most of the trouble I encounter in my work has largely to do with parents either expecting too much or too little of their children's behavior. I'm amazed at times at how much parents expect children to do and know; then I'll be amazed the next day at how little some expect. Admittedly, it's hard to find the middle road at this time in our history and in this culture, given the blurring or lack of very clear standards in so many areas. Below are some suggestions that may help you set reasonable expectations.

1. <u>Monitor your own reactions to behavior and analyze it with plain common sense.</u> Is it too much to ask that the child cease from whining or arguing every time he is asked to do a chore? Of course not. Your reaction, I'm sure, is one of irritation, perhaps righteous anger at his being so selfish and thoughtless when he is an important, valuable part of the family and should shoulder his own share of the responsibility for helping it run smoothly. Take a clue from your own feelings here. Your expectations are reasonable and good for everybody, so follow through and make sure that he does what needs doing without all the lip.

Is constant fighting, arguing and bickering between siblings something that is "normal" and impossible to stop? No, it isn't and you need to find ways to stop it from interfering with your rights to peace and quiet. You don't need to be a pediatrician to figure out that it's bad for everyone and should be managed. You can trust your instinct on so many things because there's a good chance that you were raised to be more sensitive to the needs of others, more highly socialized than many children are today. You do know what's right and wrong about how you treat others and your children need to know it, too. There is some evidence in research as well as in mine and other's experiences that show we are, as a society, raising far more self-centered, less considerate people than we did a few decades ago. I could fill a hundred more pages with depressing examples I have witnessed over the past fifteen years. Certainly we need to change that and it will happen most effectively on the parent-child level in healthy families.

2. <u>Read about children.</u> Find out what is age-appropriate behavior. There are many sources for this in librar-

ies and bookstores. You've probably already discovered the Ames and Ilg series Your (Two, Three, Four) Year Old (Dell, 1976) which I often recommend. There are hundreds of articles in magazines every year also, many in popular, accessible publications.

3. Ask other people. You might choose a family with children the age of yours, whom you see as reasonably behaving, polite children and ask the parents about your own expectations for your children. It's one of the best ways to get a real-world reading on what you're doing and how you are doing it. Of course, there are always people like me or physicians or friends who are nurses or counselors who may give you objective advice. A mother of a five year old and a strong-willed seven year old said to me this morning, "Gosh! What you're saying is just sort of common sense." I rather thought I had succeeded in getting my ideas across when she told me that.

4. Remember what is at stake if your expectations are skewed. Expecting too much or too little can be very hard on a child's growing self-esteem because the message received by her is devastating. If expectations are too high, you can produce an adult with a debilitating, chronic sense of never being quite good enough, no matter what she does. I know two women, both good friends of mine, whose main growth work involves dealing with the aftermath of being raised by fathers who could never quite be accepting of these women's best efforts. In addition to the havoc it caused them regarding their own feelings of self-worth and general life satisfaction, they're also struggling with the damage done to their relationship with dad — they resent never measuring up, they are very angry about being manipulated and demeaned by a father who never accepted

140

them as they were and are.

If the expectations are too low, on the other hand, the message is equally debilitating. Throughout this book you have read about the unspoken messages implicit in your words and actions, which children absorb before anything else you may think you are getting across. Too low expectations of children's abilities and behavior sends the message, "I don't think you can handle this" and they believe you. They become precisely what we expected them to be — underachieving, hesitant, self-doubting, "irresponsible" — and then we turn around and blame the child for what we ourselves have produced. Seems unfair, to say the very least.

Every once in a while I read some gruesome story in the newspaper about a child beaten badly or to death over some issue that often involves (in addition to the parent's own mental illness) too high expectations, such as the two year old who was beaten to death for "refusing" to close his eyes during mealtime prayers. Thank heaven those are not common; yet the potential problems that skewed expectations can bring are harmful and long-lasting. There is a middle way.

SIBLINGS AND SELF-ESTEEM

Your place in the scheme of your family had a great effect upon how you saw yourself as a child and your birth order and history with your siblings still may affect your feelings about yourself. Fate simply deals out certain hands to us over which we have no control — our size, attractiveness, intellignece, body style, economic status, etc. — which profoundly influence self-esteem, and one of those cards is who we drew as brothers and sisters. Although

I don't believe there is anything you can do to stop resentment and competition between siblings and the generally dampening effect that they have on children's positive self-perspectives, it is worth the effort here to give you perspective and suggestions which may help to ameliorate some of the negative effects of sibling hassles.

First, realize that there isn't a child alive who in her heart-of-hearts does not want to be an only child. At least I've never met one. Second, all siblings argue and fight. If you find some who don't, you've stumbled upon something never before observed. And third, consider the number of people you know (perhaps even you) who still don't get along with their brother or sister as adults and you may get some idea of why this topic is in a chapter on self-esteem.

So, what are we left with as parents when trying to manage the effects of siblings on children's self-esteem? Mostly amelioration of the strong negative messages that a child can receive from dealing with his brothers and sisters if a parent allows the conflict and rivalry to get out of hand.

GUIDELINES FOR MANAGING SIBLING CONFLICT

Your fantasy may be that the family will all get along together and you'll be able to feel loving toward them all the time. Please give that up if it's true for you, because the reality, as you know, is quadraphonic noise, dirty clothes and frayed nerves. However, most of us think it's worth it! The key word here is *management*.

1. <u>Recognize that conflict is normal, necessary and manageable.</u> You've noticed that you can't live together or work together without conflict. It is not a bad word

or a thing to be avoided, especially with children since it is in childhood that they learn, for good or ill, how to deal with it — avoid it, ignore it, bulldoze it or, hopefully, *manage* it. You will be the model for accepting and managing conflict in a creative way.

2. <u>Set an example.</u> You can show that people can get angry and disagree without resorting to violence or silence. The ways of talking and listening to your child when there is a problem or conflict that are proposed in previous chapters will show children how interpersonal disputes are resolved. Your modeling of problem solving using your listening and paraphrasing skills and I-messages tells your child in the most effective way possible what she needs to know about managing conflict. Now, what do you do when the two or three of them are right there in front of you, blaming, crying and demanding their rights?

3. <u>Act as a mediator.</u> There are steps you can quickly learn to apply in mediating disputes between siblings. Here they are:

a. <u>Ask each child to describe the problem</u> one at a time and allow *no* interruptions. Assure each that he or she will also get a turn without being interrupted. Even though it may be obvious to you what's wrong, airing out the hurt feelings and just being heard will lower the emotional level immediately.

b. <u>Have each say how they feel about it.</u> Remember you are teaching here — emotional education — and you are pulling the fuses of two or more irrational people. Being invited to tell how you feel about the whole thing works very well.

c. <u>Ask the children to offer solutions to the conflict.</u>
They may offer several solutions that you can help them
discuss and negotiate over. If they choose one that you
don't see as particularly fair or even possible, you can either
guide their thinking further or go ahead and let them try
it out. The main point is that they both have agreed to
the same plan. If it turns out that the solution they agree
on is not workable, you can always go back and repeat the
process. Keep in mind your long-term goals for your kids:
empowerment and self-confidence, the qualities that will be
vital to their success and adjustment as adults. Imposed
solutions by you will not help you reach those goals.
Sometimes you will have to impose a solution when the
children refuse to compromise, but even then, you have
learned here that their refusal is also a choice they are
making and they have to live with the consequences.

4. <u>Don't go headhunting for a villain in sibling disputes.</u>
Most often there is no clear-cut bad guy and you strain
your own credibility and waste your time by trying. If you
didn't actually see what happened, you are on shaky
ground. Assume everyone had a part in the conflict.

5. <u>Don't allow siblings to hurt each other.</u> If it gets
physical, I suggest time-out for both, followed by the
mediation described here.

6. <u>Clarify and make attractive the respective family roles,</u>
<u>privileges and responsibilities of each child.</u> Older children
tend to forget, in their hurt and resentment over being
usurped by a baby or younger sibling, that they now
have an important role — big brother or sister — and
privileges — going to school, playing away from home,

going to movies, etc. — that little sibling doesn't have. You will need to show the children the advantages of their roles by doing things with them and allowing them those privileges and by explaining the fact that one (or more) extra persons in the home mean that mom and dad have to spread their time out a little more between them.

7. Spend time one-on-one on a regular basis. You might do the dishes together or rake the yard with an individual child. You need not feel that alone time with each must be a trip for ice cream or to a movie. Some of the most satisfying times with one of my own children came when we were doing chores — insulating the attic, washing the car, moving furniture. I'm still not sure why it works that way. Do take the time. You will find it is the best prevention for left-out feelings on the part of your children (and give the child your full attention).

8. Don't insist that everything be shared. You can designate a central toy storage area for those to be shared and set aside areas for each child's private stock, making sure that the rules and reasons are clear why it is structured this way. Remember, children don't want to share their parents, let alone their toys!

9. I repeat: don't try to motivate a child by comparing her less-than-satisfactory performance to that of a sibling. This is guaranteed to backfire on you because unhappy, discouraged people don't perform well. Each child has unique and precious abilities and *styles* of doing their tasks. These should be pointed out to them and used to motivate.

10. Plan enjoyable activities (usually directed by you) that

your children can do together to help them appreciate each other in a relaxed setting. Do you remember when you and your partner "escaped" for a weekend by yourself after weeks or months of work, discipline and kids and discovered that in a different setting you were with, after all, a delightful, fun person whose other side you had not appreciated for a long time? It's a little harder each time to hate a brother or sister whom you occasionally see as a real, valuable person and not just as an obnoxious competitor.

This chapter has ranged into some rather diverse territory, hasn't it, from your own personal growth through the family factor in self-esteem to sibling rivalry? I do hope that it is clear, however, that the building blocks of a child's self-image are broad and made of diverse materials. I would rather not think of you, as parents, suddenly waking up one morning when your children are in their mid-to-late teens and saying, "My God, what happened?" Discipline, communication, confidence building, empowerment, respect, love and enhancing children's self-esteem happen every day in small ways. What you say and do the moment you put down this book will have an effect upon how your child feels about herself. You are very lucky: your children are young, enthusiastic, loving and malleable and you want to give them the best of everything — otherwise you wouldn't be on the last page of this book. Take advantage of the relatively short time you have now to love your children fully, which is really the point of all that has been written here, to enjoy their spirit, their beauty, their incomparable uniqueness, and to value your own life which you have chosen to share with them.

Good luck to you!

APPENDIX

STAYING OUT OF POWER STRUGGLES

1. Remember the child's *FEELINGS*.

2. Remain in the *ADULT EGO STATE*.

3. *REFUSE* to be trapped in *DETAILS*.

4. Put the problem back into the *CHILD'S HEAD*.

HOW WE DISCOUNT CHILDREN'S FEELINGS

1. Consider feelings as unimportant.

2. Denying that the feelings exist.

3. Listening Badly.

4. Offering advice that bypasses the feelings.

5. Defending the person the child is upset with.

6. Questioning that ignores the feelings.

HOW TO TELL CHILDREN YOU'RE UPSET

1. Say *HOW YOU FEEL.*

2. Say *WHAT BEHAVIOR IS BOTHERING YOU.*

3. Say *WHY IT BOTHERS YOU.*

4. Say *WHAT YOU WOULD LIKE CHANGED.*
   <u>Example</u>: "When you leave the lights on, I get irritated because it costs money we could use for something else. Please turn them off when you leave."

SENDING MESSAGES OF EMPOWERMENT

1. *USE FEW WORDS.*

2. *GIVE NEEDED INFORMATION.*

3. *WRITE NOTES.*

4. *TELL HOW THEIR BEHAVIOR AFFECTS YOU.*

5. *ASK FOR YOUR CHILD'S HELP SOLVING A PROBLEM.*

Super Box

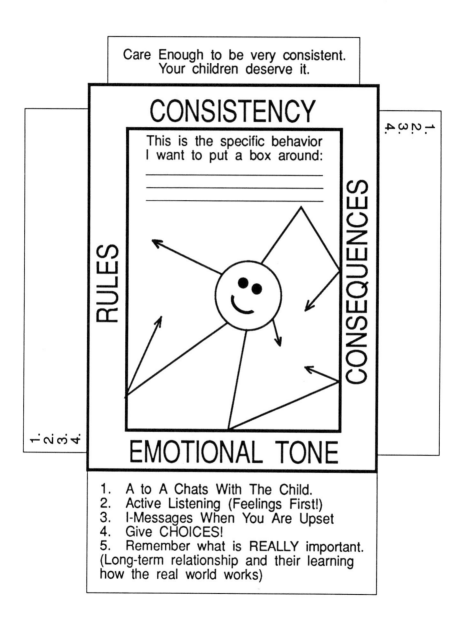

Care Enough to be very consistent.
Your children deserve it.

CONSISTENCY

This is the specific behavior
I want to put a box around:

RULES

CONSEQUENCES

EMOTIONAL TONE

1. A to A Chats With The Child.
2. Active Listening (Feelings First!)
3. I-Messages When You Are Upset
4. Give CHOICES!
5. Remember what is REALLY important.
(Long-term relationship and their learning
how the real world works)

Super Box © 1992, Jon Merritt
Permission is granted for copying for personal use.

157

Suggested Reading

Author's Note: The books listed here are among the most useful ones I have read. Some may well be out of print or hard to find but you may find them worth pursuing.

Bettleheim, Bruno, *A Good Enough Parent: A Book On Child Rearing,* Alfred A. Knopf, Inc., 1987.

Bloch, Douglas, *Words That Heal,* Bantam Books, 1988.

Bradshaw, John, *Bradshaw on: The Family: A Revolutionary Way of Self-Discovery,* Health Communications, Inc., 1988.

Bradshaw, John, *Healing The Shame That Binds You,* Health Communications, Inc., 1988.

Briggs, Dorothy, *Your Child's Self Esteem,* Dolphin Press, 1975.

Clarke, Jean Illsley, *Self Esteem: A Family Affair,* Winston Press, 1978.

Clarke, Jean Illsley and Dawson, Connie, *Growing Up Again,* © 1989 by Hazelden Foundation. Published by Harper & Row.

Cline, Foster W. and Fay, Jim, *Parenting with Love and Logic,* Navpress, 1990.

Curran, Dolores, *Traits of a Healthy Family,* Harper, 1985.

Dinkmeyer, Don and McKay, Gary, *Systematic Training for Effective Parenting,* Parent's Manual, American Guidance Services, 1984.

Dreikurs, Rudolf, *Children: The Challenge*, NAL/Dutton, 1991.

Elkind, David, *The Hurried Child*, Addison-Wesley, 1988.

Erikson, Erik, *Childhood and Society*, W.W. Norton, 1963.

Faber, Adele, and Mazlish, Elaine, *How To Talk So Kids Will Listen & Listen So Kids Will Talk*, Avon Books, 1980.

Ginott, Hiam G., *Between Parent and Child*, Avon Books, 1976.

Ginott, Hiam G., *Between Parent and Teenager*, Avon Books, 1982.

Harris, Thomas, M.D., *I'm OK, You're OK*, Avon Books, 1976.

Miller, Alice, *The Drama of the Gifted Child*, Basic Books, Inc., 1981.

Miller, Alice, *Thou Shalt Not Be Aware*, Farrar, Strauss & Giroux, Inc., 1984.

Miller, Alice, *For Your Own Good*, Farrar, Strauss & Giroux, 1984.

Peck, Scott, M.D., *The Road Less Traveled*, Simon & Schuster, 1978.

Piaget, Jean, *Six Psychological Studies*, Vintage Books, 1968.

Notes

Notes

Order Form

Additional copies of this book or Mr. Merritt's *A Parent's Primer* may be obtained by completing this order form and sending it along with a check or money order payable to:

Parenting Resources Publications
2803 S.W. Hume Court
Portland, OR 97219

Order No.	Qty	Title	Unit Cost	Total
120170		Empowering Children	8.95	
111571		A Parent's Primer	8.95	

	Subtotal	
	Shipping & Handling *(see chart at left)*	
	TOTAL	

Shipping & Handling Charges

Amount of Order	Charges
$0.00 - $10.00	$2.50
$10.01 - $25.00	$3.50
$25.01 - $50.00	$4.00
$50.01 - $75.00	$5.00

Send Books To

Name_____

Address_____

City_____ State_____ Zip_____

No cash or C.O.D.'s please. Quantity discounts are available.
Allow 2 weeks for delivery.